Advance Praise for *Hello Emotions!*

"To be honest, the self-improvement category is not my favorite genre as I prefer reading natural science, politics, or history. However, reading *Hello Emotions!* made me realize that the most intricate and interesting place to explore is not in the lab, out in the universe, or in the past. It is within ourselves, where emotions, the main characters of this book, exist. Thao and Dan have done a wonderful job mapping a community of 27 emotions we all experience regularly. Those emotions are so alive that sometimes I felt like I was watching an extended version of Disney's well-known movie *Inside Out*.

"These remarkable stories make it easy to clarify what leaves us feeling fulfilled or miserable. Thao and Dan's approach is very simple: You should name things before trying to resolve or shift them. After finishing *Hello Emotions!*, I became more mindful about myself, especially whenever I have unpleasant feelings. I can immediately detect which among the community of emotions is challenging me, then say hello and look for a way to create harmony. It's such an interesting experience!"

—Le Hoang Thach
CEO at Voiz FM Vietnam

"I have struggled with emotions. When still young, I had come to the conclusion that there were negative and positive emotions, and that showing 'negative' emotions such as anger, disappointment, or sadness was a weakness. So, I grew up hiding my emotions. I wanted to prove I was a strong woman!

"That was fine for many years until I began to feel an unexplained emptiness. There was something stuck in my head that I could not explain. Some days tears kept coming, but I didn't know why. I did not understand myself. That's when I started to realize the importance of the messages behind these emotions.

"This book, which is the combination of Thao's stories, shared in her blog over the past two years, and Dan's meaningful lessons and wisdom, has helped me understand. This book has become a guide for the journey of finding myself.

"I love the way Thao uses the metaphor of ourselves as a house and emotions as visitors. They visit us to give us a message that triggers certain actions. Nothing positive or negative about them—they are all trying to help us. So, instead of welcoming only selected visitors and ignoring others, I have learnt to welcome them all to my house and to listen to their stories with compassion and less judgment. That is sometimes difficult, but the result is always interesting.

"Sometimes, Stress visits me, but after reflection, I realize Fear of Judgment is the one sending the message. Passion comes and goes, but when combined with Enthusiasm helps me to be more resilient and even impacts the risk I'm willing to take.

"Now, I spend at least ten minutes a day reflecting, cleaning, and preparing my house so my emotional friends are comfortable visiting and open to sharing with me. The more I embrace my emotions, the more I understand myself, the more mature I am, and the more ready I am to face upcoming challenges in the journey ahead.

"Thanks, Thao and Dan, for a very valuable book. I hope this book becomes a guide for your journey to discover and fall in love with your emotions."

—Anh Bui
Learning and Development Manager at Nestlé Vietnam

"What a great book about the role of emotions in our world! These true-to-life stories are a touching and helpful way to reflect on why an emotion shows up and how we might come to understand it. Whether an emotion seems positive or negative, it always has our best interest at heart. The more we respect emotions, the more we see their power. I hope you'll enjoy reading it as much as I have and that it will redefine the role of emotions in your life."

—Ngan Nguyen
HR Manager at Suntory PepsiCo Vietnam

"*Hello Emotions!* has become a peaceful and wise friend that has a home on my night table. It is perfect reading at the close of the day, at night before I sleep, or at dawn for a bright start to the day.

"Thao's stories speak volumes to the hidden emotional friends that I rarely take the chance to converse with because of the busyness of my corporate life. Even though I am familiar with her stories, they still feel fresh and provocative each time I read them. The emotions she writes about befriending—anxiety, gratitude, happiness, nostalgia—come alive and speak to me.

"Thao's writing is simple, endearingly vivid, and enlightening in a way that provokes deep reflection and curiosity about the lessons I could absorb. Her ability to translate daily conversations and events into wise observations and practical lessons about emotions is exactly the reason you should read this book over and over! Trust me that every single chapter is a lesson on its own, and you don't want to miss a thing!"

—Hoang-Anh Do
Talent and Organization Consulting, Abbott Vietnam

My immediate reaction was "OMG I love this book!" It was easy to read and had wonderful examples that helped clarify a variety of every-day emotions in real-life experiences. I found myself scrolling in anticipation to see what emotion you had selected next. (How DID you decide which emotions to choose??)"

To those considering reading *Hello Emotions!*, I would share that the authors do a masterful job of conveying the key features of emotions through story-telling and clear framing of the way emotions work through us. As a coach, I can't wait to share this with my clients!

—Kim Ebinger
Executive Coach

"In my many years of working in the field of human development, I have rarely read a more accessible book on the topic of emotions than *Hello Emotions!* by Thao and Dan. The stories by Thao bring emotions to life in clear, practical, and entertaining ways, while Dan's commentary provides additional context, depth, and clarity. I am sure this book will support its readers in gaining greater access to and competence with the world of emotions."

—Curtis Watkins
MCC and Co-author of *The Field Guide to Emotions*

"*Hello Emotions!* is a delightful book to read when you are feeling lost and trying to make sense of your feelings. I find the many mini-stories shared by Thao very inspiring and relatable. I really enjoyed the poetic style that Thao adopted, and it made reading the book entertaining and thought-provoking.

"Dan's narrative of the emotions provides helpful insights into the many emotions that we experience but cannot quite place or understand. When we clarify what our emotions are telling us, we can leverage them to move us forward and find outcomes that we never could have anticipated. I would recommend *Hello Emotions!* to anyone who is keen to understand their own emotions and those of other people so that they can better navigate the delicate and intricate web of human interactions."

—Rosalind Wong
Executive and Life Coach

"*Hello Emotions!* is an interesting and enjoyable 'stories' book for anyone and everyone. The authors have brought *Emotions* to life in a way that I could imagine having an open conversation with them as well.

"I used to believe that having emotions was bad and not professional. It was also a sign of weakness when we showed our emotions. I always hid them whenever I could.

"After reading the stories, I started to realize that these *Emotions* are friends with others as well. I did not know the *Emotions'* names until the authors described their behaviors and characteristics. Those experiences resonated deeply with me and reminded me that I was not alone. These *Emotions* are so friendly to everyone—they will visit us at any time of the day when we call out to them. After naming each of these *Emotion* friends, I started to embrace them instead of rejecting them.

"Now, I show more compassion to both my *Emotions* and myself; I no longer see them as right or wrong, positive or negative. I am not afraid to tell people that these *Emotions* are my friends.

"Not all friends are enjoyable to be with; however, they do have some value to bring to the table. The realization and tips shared in the book allow me to navigate my mood and emotions. I hope to strengthen my emotional muscles and continue to choose when and who to invite into my house. I now have a door I can open."

—Peh Puay Eng, Life and Career Coach
Training and Development Facilitator

"The older I get, the clumsier I become with 'emotions,' a friendly concept that seems too familiar to think of as something hard to handle. Contrary to the belief I held through my years as a teenager (how naïve I was!), there are times when my emotions seem as complex as rocket science, so I give up trying to deal with them and shift my attention elsewhere.

"That was true until I came across Thao and Dan's book, which has guided my journey to unbox and befriend my emotions.

This book has all the essence of what I have found 'magical' in my experience: elaborate storytelling through which emotions and what they are offering us are effortlessly unveiled.

"In these stories, I believe you will experience many 'Aha!' moments. You will see yourself in these stories and gain insights from the way Thao and Dan reveal each emotion, what it means, and what questions to ask and reflect on when it emerges.

"Their explanation of how some emotions can be mistaken for each other is also very thoughtful, and makes this a deeply enjoyable and pleasant piece to read. This book is something I wish I'd had available during my early twenties, as it would have allowed me to embark more preparedly into adulthood."

—Giang Nguyen
Brand Manager at Unilever Vietnam

HELLO EMOTIONS!

Stories of Befriending Emotions

Thao Pham and Dan Newby

Printed and bound in the United States of America
ISBN: 978-1-7324509-6-7

SPECIAL THANKS!

Some stories about our emotional friends were translated from the Vietnamese version by Trinh Nguyen. The authors wish to gratefully acknowledge Trinh for her generous assistance in translation, Frank Steele for his excellent editing job, Stefan Merour for our wonderful book design, and especially illustrator Cuong Nguyen for helping us bring our emotional friends into life.

DEDICATION

This book is dedicated to my grandmother (Nghiem Pham), my father (Dau Pham), and my mother (Tu Nguyen), who presented me a peaceful childhood, and to my nephew (Khoi Pham) and my lovely niece (Thi Pham), who have colored my life.—Thao

I dedicate this book to my parents, Don and Maybelle, who lit the fire of learning early in my life, and to my wife, Lucy, who is a daily inspiration and support.—Dan

TABLE OF CONTENTS

PART 3: A FEW MORE FUN OBSERVATIONS ABOUT OUR SPECIAL FRIENDS

FOREWORD

What we can understand is what we can deal with.

We take emotions for granted when they suit us. As we are happy, we simply want the sensations of delight, fulfillment, and peace to last forever. We run away from emotions when they don't suit us. As we are sad, we just want to escape this empty and irritating state as soon as possible.

Worst of all, we sometimes ignore our emotions and let them control our temper, our days, and eventually our destiny.

Multiple neuroscience and psychology studies have found that emotions drive our actions much more than we realize. The mechanism is subtle yet powerful. While logic and rationality take time to work, emotions quickly guide us toward actions. Their efficiency lies in the fact that each emotion comes with an established story in our mind. When an emotion is triggered, its story is recalled and our brain quickly relies on past experiences to find an immediate way to react. Some stories have been formed for millions of years and are coded in our genes. Other stories are shaped by our own interactions with the world.

Hello Emotions!

Our struggle with emotions usually comes from our ignorance or misunderstanding of their stories. While we are taught extensively at school about how the external world functions, we are very ill-equipped to deal with our internal world of emotions. As aligning ourselves with our environment is critical for adaptation and growth, the more we can understand our emotions, the more we can make them work for us and live a meaningful and successful life in whatever way we define.

Thao and Dan's book *Hello Emotions!* uncovers the stories behind 27 popular emotions. Each story is vividly illustrated by Thao's personal experiences. I've known Thao for years both as a top-notch kick-ass professional and later as a dedicated coach, courageous entrepreneur, and Buddhism practitioner. Through her career transition, she managed to keep the same qualities that make her excel: a brilliant mind and a devotion to helping others. When she understands something, she gets to the gist of it and finds a clear way to articulate it for others. In this book, Thao offers her own vulnerabilities, deepest thoughts, and bare soul. Her reflections and analysis shed light on our blurry world of emotions and help us appreciate what it has to offer.

Dan's recaps of each emotion give us an objective and balanced viewpoint. We learn that the seemingly bad emotions may actually come with good intentions, and the seemingly good emotions can be cultivated internally and manifested many times if we pay attention. As a master of the topic, he teaches us practical and timeless techniques to live in harmony with emotions. For readers who are familiar with his two previous brilliant books on emotions, I am sure you will find his new book another insightful and enjoyable read.

All readers can probably find a bit of themselves in the authors' narratives. It's common for us to get trapped in loneliness, drown in envy, or be scrambled by anxiety. What I hope is that by the end of this book, we are all set to figure out our way to play with "loneliness," tame "envy," and train "anxiety." Once we've understood the underlying mechanism of emotions, we are free to write our own stories.

Thao Huong Vu
Head of Marketing at BAEMIN VN

Part 1

INTRODUCTION

A NOTE FROM THAO

Friends of mine often wonder why a "rational" person like me, who was always at the top of her mathematics class, graduated with a Silver medal from the University of Technology, worked in the world of research for more than a decade, and was occupied with numbers from morning until night suddenly fell in love with emotions so deeply.

That simple question has led to days of contemplation. Every time I sat in front of my laptop, ready to write down my thoughts, all the words ran away. They were scared of the dozens of questions flooding my mind. "When did I start learning about emotions? What made me curious about them? Why did I never think about the emotional world when I was a child? How did I survive without understanding them?" and many more.

I sat, looking at the computer screen, not knowing where to begin. Should I go back to my childhood when the little me believed the world was so peaceful or should I start from the stage where I found this life so intense? In the end, the logical part in me made the decision. It demanded a chronological story.

Hello Emotions!

I was a normal kid with a normal childhood. It was so normal that I am always envious of those who can tell stories about the "exciting" events in their childhood. Cutting class, teasing the neighboring dogs till they barked loudly, ringing the neighbors' doorbells and then running away. I wish I had something dramatic like that to impress my nephew and niece. My childhood was extraordinarily peaceful. I was accompanied on my walk to kindergarten in the morning and returned home for lunch. After taking a nap, I spent the whole afternoon arranging seashells, soil, leaves, and flowers, pretending that I was selling food in my restaurant. Every day repeated itself until the day I learned about spelling and became a bookworm.

All the others in my circle of friends seem to have shared a similar childhood. We were obedient kids, good students, and teachers' pets. We competed to get a high ranking in natural science subjects such as Mathematics, Physics, and Chemistry. Our good results never failed to please our parents and teachers, who believed that this would lead the next generations to a brighter future.

They were right; my future was very bright. I was loved by my teachers, graduated from top schools, and chose to work in fields related to what I had mastered. I received offers to join multinational companies thanks to my good grades in natural science subjects and logical reasoning. During those first thirty-something years, I only "hung out" with numbers. Emotions were something foreign, which never existed in any of my memories, and I felt like I was a kite.

A note from Thao

My kite did not always fly as fast or as high as the other kites, but every year it flew a little higher, and over time it surpassed all my expectations. Occasionally, it was shaken a bit by unpredictable air currents, but regained its balance and boldly moved forward.

The day it all changed, the sky was clear and I was flying high when suddenly thunder rumbled and lightning struck. Around me, all the other kites were in a panic. After a few minutes, someone crashed into me and everything went blank. Darkness blanketed the sky. I lost my way, wobbled, and lost hope.

I did not know what was going on inside me or how to express myself to get help. My mind was jammed with negative thoughts. The "emotions" which I usually named were Emptiness and Stress. In retrospect, they were a bundle of unpleasant emotions, including Resentment, Anger, Disappointment, Hate, Anxiety, Fear, Boredom, Hopelessness, and Despair.

During those stormy days, the only place I could find Peace was in Thay Thich Nhat Hanh's books, and I started learning Mindfulness from them. Little by little the Mindfulness practice helped calm my unsettled mind and healed my suffering. I stopped denying and running away from the emotions I labeled "negative." Through Thay's teachings, they became very close and dear.

Mindfulness practice was like sunshine, lightening the darkness surrounding me. For the first time, I began "seeing" clearly all the emotional friends who had been staying in my house for so long. I learned to embrace and take care of unpleasant emotions during meditation sessions. They all dissipated as I breathed. Yet the moment I was back in my normal life, some of the difficult emotions returned and lingered, trying to say something I could not understand, and that made me curious.

On my journey to explore the world of emotions, I "met" another great teacher, Dan Newby. Dan's wonderful articulation of each emotion's message, impulse, and purpose was a huge surprise. Returning home from Dan's training classes, I could "hear" what my emotional friends had to say and they could understand me too. It was a sheer delight!

My emotional friends and I started having meaningful conversations, which have given me countless insights into myself, more internal solidity, and more resilience during the storms in my life. To my surprise, I did not turn into someone less logical by hanging around with emotions, but became more logical when making decisions thanks to the additional source of information I get from these friends.

Each short story in this book tells one of my personal experiences on my journey to understand the emotional world. They were created out of my knowledge, reflection, and practical experience. I hope you will find something interesting and learn to love your emotions as I do mine.

A NOTE FROM DAN

Each of us ultimately develops a unique relationship with emotions. This relationship is shaped by our biology, of course, but also by the multitude of experiences that constitute our lives. From these experiences we learn, not just cognitively but also emotionally. We may become more prudent or more adventurous, more compassionate, or more anxious.

In this book, we invite you to reflect on the relationship you have developed with emotions. It is fundamental to any journey that we know where we are starting. If we don't, we will not have any idea which direction to proceed or what steps to take to get where we want to go. Understanding your current relationship with emotions positions the "you are here" dot on the map of emotions.

One of the most important aspects of your inquiry is that you strive to be non-judgmental—of yourself, of emotions, of others. The question isn't whether you like the emotions you discover, but that you view them clearly. Once you do, you'll be able to choose a direction to grow emotionally. It may not be a rapid journey, but we can assure you it will be satisfying.

Hello Emotions!

Embracing your emotions makes you "comfortable in your own skin" and brings peace to the seemingly incessant wrestling that takes place between your thinking and feeling, between reason and emotion. You may discover, as we have, that there is not as much value in the conflict as there is in the two learning to dance together and support each other. Welcome to the journey of emotional self-discovery.

HOW TO READ THIS BOOK

This book emerged from the shared passion and respect the authors have for emotions. Yet it was crafted by authors who learned about emotions a world apart in widely disparate cultures. What is evident from this collaboration is that emotions are a universal human attribute and that there are a variety of ways we can understand and live them.

Thao's stories capture the lyricism and beauty of her world, Dan's reflections and analysis provide a pragmatic articulation of the befriended emotions.

The order of the stories evolved organically and we have kept them as they emerged and knocked on Thao's "door". The emotions appearing first were those "who" demanded her attention immediately at the beginning of her journey into the world of emotions. After she came to understand their messages and have meaningful conversations with them, she could "see" and "listen" to more subtle emotions. These included Nostalgia, Envy, Hate, along with other pleasant friends such as Acceptance, Peace, Joy, Gratitude. Thus, the sequence of the stories follows Thao's exploration of her emotional world. The emotions are listed in alphabetical order in the Table of Contents for easy search with the page number on which they begin which will lead you to the emotion for which you are searching.

This book is intended to provoke you to question the way you've come to understand emotions and to consider how else you might relate to them. It is designed to be the beginning of a journey and not a summary of all you can learn about emotions.

Read, enjoy, reflect, question, consider. Viewing the book through these lenses will allow you to gain the most from it.

We are grateful you are joining us as we journey together to discover all that we've overlooked about our emotions and their role in our lives.

Thao and Dan

Part 2

HELLO!
WELCOME TO OUR
CIRCLE OF FRIENDS

DISAPPOINTMENT

Disappointment is a girl with a rich imagination, picky and demanding. Any time she is dissatisfied, she tattles to her brother, Anger. Never mind whether Disappointment is right or wrong, Anger always keenly and belligerently punishes the other party in no time.

Hello Emotions!

A few years ago, I traveled to Japan with a friend. After a few days, my friend developed a serious allergic reaction. Her skin became more and more itchy and red every day. She neither had health insurance nor wanted to pay for the expensive health care in Japan, so she changed her ticket and flew home earlier than our original plan. I was left in Japan with seven more days ahead. While wondering what to do, I remembered a Vietnamese former colleague who was currently studying in Japan. In her farewell letter to me she had written, "Tell me when you come to Japan."

Bursting with Joy, I texted her, asking where she was so I could pay a visit. Message sent, text read, yet her reply only came after half a day. A few more messages repeated the same pattern and quickly consumed a few days, but no meeting time was decided. Needless to say, Anger was my companion in the following days and carefully advised, "Forget this relationship! What a friend!" Later, any time I saw her posts on Facebook, Hate subtly whispered, "Unfollow or block her! How irritating!"

A few years later, I received a text from former colleagues in the Philippines:

"Thao, my boss and I are traveling to Vietnam. We are so excited to see you again!"

"Welcome to my country! I am excited too! Where are you traveling to? Where will you stay? Any plans yet?"

"We have no plan, we just want to visit Ho Chi Minh City."

Disappointment

"Ho Chi Minh City does not have many tourist attractions. It's good to stay here for a day or two; after that, you two had better visit other wonderful places in my country."

"No, we just would like to visit you."

"Have you booked a hotel yet?"

No response.

A few weeks later, she texted me again, still with no answer to my last question. I then realized that my former colleagues expected me to be their host during their stay. My working schedule was tight, and my tiny one-bedroom apartment was not an ideal accommodation.

I felt myself stuck in a predicament. I suddenly chuckled, recalling my own experience in Japan. I laughed at myself because I had created just such a predicament for another person and then felt angry at that person. In that moment, a lesson from my coach training program that I had taken for granted flashed through my mind:

"You don't have to make a commitment to doing something if you don't promise."

It is obvious that we have the right to deny people's requests which we deem unreasonable. Why would we be responsible for what we have never committed to?

My former Vietnamese colleague only told me to "tell her" when I came to Japan, but my imagination envisioned her spending time with me, hosting me, and hanging out with me when I visited Japan. I then believed my expectation was her promise; consequently I became disappointed, angry, and hated her when my expectations were not met.

Likely, when I said to my Filipino colleagues, "Tell me when you visit Vietnam," I intended to enjoy some dinners and sightseeing with them if my schedule allowed, but I did not plan for a weeklong accommodation. I breathed a sigh of relief as I felt the pressure taken off my chest. I texted my former colleague saying clearly that I could only arrange some times to meet for dinner, sent her a list of tourist attractions, hotels, and good restaurants for her reference, and said that I was looking forward to seeing them again.

My colleague was silent and did not pursue her trip to Vietnam. I don't know if she was upset, since she still Facebook-tagged me in our old photos. It was the first time I overcame such a predicament without feeling guilty because of the thought, "I will disappoint other people if I don't meet their expectation." I was also glad that I hadn't done anything to damage my relationship with my Vietnamese colleague in Japan. We are still in good contact.

▶ *Have you ever gotten angry at someone because you were disappointed?*

▶ *What were your expectations of that person? Did they promise something they didn't do or was your expectation just something you imagined?*

▶ *What could you do to reduce the frequency of Disappointment's visits?*

DAN'S THOUGHTS

Disappointment is such a fascinating emotion. We misunderstand it in several ways. The first is that we often believe it means "something is wrong." When we do, our first reaction is to blame someone or something for being the cause. When we are disappointed with ourselves, we turn our blame inward.

But if you pick apart a simple situation where you felt disappointment, you'll see that what produced the disappointment was a gap between your expectations and reality. You were thinking you would go hiking and have a picnic, but when you got up in the morning, it was raining torrentially. Your expectation can't be fulfilled because of the weather. You may not like the situation, but that does not mean something is inherently wrong with it. It just isn't aligned with your expectations.

How disappointment between people occurs is interesting to consider. Others may tell us we have disappointed them, but what occurs most often is that they have created an expectation that we don't fulfill. If we have made a promise that becomes the basis of their expectation, then we are culpable; but if we have not made a commitment, the responsibility for the disappointment rests squarely with them. And the reverse is true, of course, which is why it is valuable to ask ourselves whether our disappointment is based on an unfulfilled promise or it stems from an expectation we invented in the hope the other person would do what we wanted.

If we want to navigate disappointment with less suffering, we can begin by (1) recognizing that we are feeling disappointment, (2) checking our expectations—were they our invention or was a promise made to us? and (3) deciding what we need to do to realign our expectations with reality. Generally, the first step is acceptance of the gap, followed by a bit of creativity to create a new plan

---

Disappointment

Story: "This isn't what I expected."
Impulse: To look for the disconnect
Purpose: Align our expectations with reality

Source: *The Field Guide to Emotions* by Dan Newby and Curtis Watkins.

ANGER

Anger is the big brother in the family of emotions. Wherever injustice or wrongdoings occur, he shows up. Once Anger has decided what is wrong or unjust, he looks for someone to punish.

Anger was my partner in crime for decades. We were so close that for a long time I believed that its aggressiveness was part of my God-given nature.

Hello Emotions!

With Anger by my side, I wasn't afraid of anyone. Once Anger and I teamed up to fight for justice, we never cared about the status or importance of the other person. My determination was without limits. I was not dissuaded by the possible consequences of my actions, even if it meant being fired.

Until the time Anger brought me notoriety. My intimate friends and colleagues knew that my intentions were good and that my heart was kind, only that I had a quick temper; but my other relationships gradually eroded. Guilt started visiting me more often. That was when I started questioning the presence of Anger in my life.

Rumor had it that Compassion could mediate Anger. But how could I have compassion for someone who made me so angry? In the middle of my burning madness, considering the idea "Don't be mad! Be compassionate!" sounded like throwing fuel on the fire.

I searched Zen master Thich Nhat Hanh's books (hereinafter referred to as Thay, meaning "master" in Vietnamese). I read one book after another looking for the answer, but I still could not understand how to generate Compassion. One day, while reading Thay's book *At Home in the World*, my mind was shaken by a simple story, "Call Me by My True Names."

The story told of Thay hearing about a small ship carrying boat people being attacked by pirates. An eleven-year-old girl was raped. Her father tried to save her but he was thrown into the sea. After being raped, she jumped into the ocean and drowned herself. Anger visited Thay that night.

Anger

In his meditation, Thay imagined himself being born into a very poor fishing family living in deprivation. He would never have gotten a chance to go to school. His parents wouldn't have been able to read or write. They would not know how to raise their kids properly and had been poor for many generations. Growing up, he would have followed the adults in his community to the sea and learned to rob to survive. He would have acted as others did without knowing what was right or wrong. Thay came to realize that being angry or punishing the pirate would not solve the root of the problem. The Anger vanished and only his Compassion remained.

At that time, I couldn't have Compassion for the pirates like Thay did, but the story shook me. I came to realize how much privilege I had been born into and that I'd been raised in a nurturing environment. If I had been born in a poor fishing village, I would have grown up seeing the world as the pirates did.

That day I sat in silence for a long time recalling all the people whom I have been mad at and punished. By trying to put myself in their shoes, naturally, past situations presented new perspectives.

My team member submitted her report late because she was new to the job and I was too busy to give her a detailed explanation. My research partners did not deliver a useful analysis with actionable recommendations because they did not have the full picture of my company brand's performance nor access to our internal data. Only I knew the details, thanks to numerous discussions with the marketing team. My boss pressured and rushed the whole team to work until midnight because she was under constant pressure from above.

It was the first time I realized that there is always more than one option whenever Anger visits. I can blindly follow Anger's slogan, "This is unjust," and immediately punish the perpetrator, thereby generating a lot of negative energy. Or, I can pause for a moment, put myself in the shoes of others to assess if what happened is truly unjust, then search for a solution to address the root issues. That would be the way to transform the energy of Anger into Compassion.

▶ *Does Anger visit you quite often?*

▶ *What does Anger tell you is wrong or unjust?*

▶ *If you were in the other person's position, how would you view this "wrong" or "unjust" situation? Then what could be the path to bring back justice?*

DAN'S THOUGHTS

Of all the so-called "negative emotions," anger is among the most common. One reason is that it is powerful and we often feel at its mercy. We struggle to control it but find we usually cannot. Another reason is that we use the word anger as a catchall, like a basket, where we mix up many related emotions. We may feel frustration, disappointment, ire, annoyance, impatience, or aggravation, yet call it anger. So not all "anger" is anger.

Many people are scared of anger—their own or the anger of others. That is because the impulse of anger is to punish. This desire to punish has logic to it. Anger is provoked when we believe something unjust is being done to us or someone we care about. Often the quickest way to get it to stop is by confronting the perpetrator.

One tendency some people have developed is to try repressing anger. They deny it, rationalize it, or run away from it. Anger suppressed often morphs into resentment. We may believe it is too direct to say something is unjust, but we can say it is unfair. When we feel resentment we have the impulse to "get even" or take revenge for the unfairness we perceive.

Anger is one of the emotions that is most effectively handled through navigation. That means instead of reacting, which often doesn't remove the injustice, crafting a more effective and appropriate response. Counting to ten, biting your tongue, closing your computer, or smiling and walking away are ways to give yourself the time needed to move from reacting to responding.

This is one of the precepts of mindfulness. When we remain aware of the forces at play, internal and external, we can adapt moment to moment. An entry point to presence can be through the breath. There are many techniques that increase our focus, presence, and awareness so that we can act in concert with our deepest values.

Anger is provoked not by something *being* unjust, but by our *belief* that something is unjust. Simply imagining a situation where someone might betray us can provoke anger. Given that, we should verify our beliefs and be careful not to jump to conclusions. Our story seems true to us but is not The Truth. There are always multiple perspectives, but we can easily forget that.

Many times we'll find that if we consider the way the other person sees the situation, our anger evaporates. We can put ourselves in the shoes of the other person by sincerely asking ourselves, "What did they intend?" or "Were they aware?" A helpful question is whether we truly want to understand the other person or would we rather hold on to our anger and feel righteous? Which will serve us better in the long run?

If we remember that anger allows us to distinguish what we believe is just from what is unjust, it serves as a moral compass and is an enormously important emotion. Learning to navigate it will put it at our service; otherwise, it may try to take the lead. Befriending anger will change your view of and relationship with this essential emotion.

Anger

Story: "This is unjust or morally wrong."
Impulse: Stop the injustice or punish the source
Purpose: To highlight what we believe is unjust and, by extension, what we believe is just

---

Source: "The Field Guide to Emotions" by Dan Newby and Curtis Watkins

RESENTMENT

Resentment is the fraternal twin of Anger. But, unlike Anger, he is reticent and discreet. Unfairness is what he cannot stand. On his face, it seems nothing is going on, but below the surface an explosion is waiting to be released. Sometimes Resentment is triggered in one place and explodes in another. Sometimes he saves a few charges to explode at once. His destruction can be massive.

Though they look alike, it is quite easy to distinguish the twin brothers when they show up. Anger allows us to release our energy immediately, whereas Resentment urges us to bury it inside ourselves, often because we believe we don't have the power to change the situation.

Resentment's motto is "It shouldn't be this way. This is unfair. I shouldn't have suffered this."

My resentment used to be directed toward a very special "person"—God.

Hello Emotions!

It was a year-end day enfolded in the tranquillity of New Year's Eve. Resentment sat next to me moaning, "I've been on this coaching journey for so long! I'm nearly exhausted, yet my destination still seems out of reach. My dream wasn't so big. I only hoped that when I got here, Anxiety would stop pestering me for a stable monthly income. If you ask me why I am feeling this way, I only have to compare my situation with the one I had in the corporate world. I did not feel I had a meaningful impact on people's lives like I do now, but I lived a comfortable life and didn't worry about earning a living. Life is so unfair!"

Resentment started crying. I let him cry until he was exhausted and then asked: "Are you sure you are contributing to society more than in the past?"

"Uhm … actually … I am not certain. In the past, though I didn't help very many people transform their lives like I am doing now as a coach, I always made generous monthly donations to a few not-for-profit organizations, which I am not able to do now." That startled

Resentment

Resentment. He left when he realized that what he believed was unfair couldn't be justified.

After some reflection, I called on Boldness to help me plan for the next leg of my journey: designing the life I've always dreamed of. In that plan, I would allow myself to do what brought me joy and what I believed was right without paying attention to Anxiety until there were no savings left in my bank account. When that time came, if I had to go back to my old journey, I would willingly accept it.

Boldness and I executed our plan. Every time we went to meet clients, both of us were upfront about what we could and could not do and that the clients' engagement and support were vital for their project's success. I first thought that sharing the limitations of our coaching and training tools would backfire on us, but our authenticity eventually won trust and earned us more contracts.

Being unable to make substantial regular donations to causes like I had before, I started a fundraising campaign leveraging my coaching that has been warmly welcomed by my clients. I'm happy to be busy and helpful, and my clients are happy too, because they not only achieve their coaching goals but also get fulfillment from supporting charitable organizations.

The energy of Resentment has been transformed into Boldness and Fulfillment.

▶ *Has Resentment ever visited you?*
▶ *What does Resentment tell you is unfair?*
▶ *Is it really unfair when you see it from a different angle? Then what will you do to transform his energy?*

DAN'S THOUGHTS

Stop for a moment and make a short list of things you feel are unfair in your life. You might think, "I shouldn't have to do x," or "I should be able to do y." Often we can recognize resentment because it is verbalized using the words "should" or "shouldn't."

While we may picture a resentful person as bitter and bad-tempered, we all feel this emotion at times, and it has a lovely purpose. Just as anger helps us identify what we believe is just and unjust, resentment helps us identify what we believe is fair and unfair.

I find the concept of fairness intriguing. Some people confuse fairness, or "what is equitable," with "things being equal." Here's a personal example. My wife loves *linguine alle vongole*. It is a simple Italian pasta that features clams. Each time she prepares it, she counts out the clams to be sure we each receive an equal number. She considers this fair. I do not. Since I'm significantly larger than her, I believe that we should divide the clams based on our relative size. She does not. So, you can see that we differ in our assessment of what is fair. It depends on our criteria for fairness or our standard.

I could become resentful if I dwelled on her way of dividing the clams, but I prefer to select a different emotion. I usually opt for love. I know that she loves clams more than I do and I can see the satisfaction it gives her to have an equal number of clams, so I have given up the argument that it isn't fair. In this case, I've adopted her interpretation out of love.

Confusion often arises when we try to distinguish "injustice" from "unfairness." The word "just" derives from a Latin root that speaks about "a moral principle." So, believing something is "just" is equivalent to seeing it as morally correct. Fairness does not have a moral implication. In the vongole example above, there is no suggestion that anyone is a good or bad person, simply that we see what is fair differently.

Many great societal debates are centered on what we believe is morally right and wrong, or just and unjust. In most societies killing another person is considered unjust and morally wrong, yet in times of war, some people will find a way to justify it, while others will not. So, we will see some people fighting out of patriotism and others resisting as pacifists. This isn't just a question of fairness or unfairness, but what we consider morally right and wrong behavior.

This confusion between injustice and unfairness is exacerbated in languages that do not have separate words for "just" and "fair" as English does. Partly this is the historical consequence of English words deriving sometimes from Latin and other times from Old English or Northern European roots. *Iustus* is the Latin root of "just," fæger is the Old English root of "fair." They are similar concepts but still distinct.

Resentment

Story: "It shouldn't be like this; this is unfair; I shouldn't have to do this."

Impulse: To resist and get even for the perceived unfairness

Purpose: Identify what we believe is fair and unfair

Source: "The Field Guide to Emotions" by Dan Newby and Curtis Watkins

ANXIETY

Anxiety and Fear are another set of twins. Their faces are identical and their manners are largely similar.

Anxiety's favorite slogan is "I believe something may harm me, but I'm not sure what it might be," while Fear's motto is "I believe something may harm me, and I'm clear what it is."

Hello Emotions!

For me, Anxiety is more disturbing than Fear. The most frightening part is that she is unclear what the threat is. Without understanding the root issue, it is impossible to find the solution. She follows me and makes me anxious day after day.

When I switched to the coaching realm, I started meeting senior management at high-profile multinational corporations more often. To bring coaching tools to the companies' team development agenda, I first needed to help these leaders understand the usefulness of these tools.

One day, after meeting with the CEO of a famous fast-food chain, I left the meeting feeling exhausted. All my energy was drained. My brain had stopped working due to the intensity of the discussion. I heard Hate complaining:

"I hate these meetings. I wish I could dedicate all my energy just to coaching and training clients."

Anxiety continued:

"Precisely! I was anxious to prepare my presentation the whole day before. Then I was nervous and tense for several hours in the conference room dealing with difficult questions. It is ten times more tiring than teaching or coaching clients."

Finally, the penny dropped. Anxiety was the one depleting all my energy. Holding Anxiety's hand, I gently asked:

"Anxiety, what worries you so much?"

"If we do not prepare the presentation carefully, we will not be able to answer all the questions. If we cannot answer, the client will think we are incompetent and will not sign the contract. Consequently, you will not have the chance to train, coach, and do the work you love."

"Not being able to do what I love" was Anxiety's key concern, causing her to follow and unnerve me days and nights before every meeting with potential customers.

Giving up a ten-year career to switch to coaching was not a trivial matter, and not being able to do the job I loved was indeed scary. But, I also realized that my mission was to help, not to sell. If my work didn't benefit others, then I shouldn't continue.

Since then, "helping, not selling" has become my mindset when meeting new clients. With the mission of helping, I ask more questions, listen more to understand the challenges that these business leaders are facing, learn about their goals, and honestly share my approach to see if it meets their expectations. If both sides are satisfied and agree to support each other, we will then proceed. If we do not find common ground at that moment, we will wait for the moment when we do.

I learned a great lesson that day. Anxiety's purpose isn't to make me nervous. Her mission is to help me understand deeply what I treasure the most and what I am most scared of losing. She is urging me to have a solution to manage that risk or to prepare myself to embrace Courage if the worst happens.

> ▶ *Does Anxiety often pay you a visit?*
> ▶ *What is the possible danger she is trying to show you?*
> ▶ *What is your action plan to manage the risk? And are you ready for the worst to happen?*

DAN'S THOUGHTS

Anxiety is a common emotion that most of us feel several times daily. But, like anger, we refer to many emotions that are not anxiety using this label. So sometimes "anxiety" isn't anxiety.

Imagine you are crossing a parking lot in the company of a five-year-old child. You will probably instinctively want to hold their hand. Your senses will be on alert for cars that might back out of their parking space and endanger the child. This is anxiety doing its job. The role of anxiety is to keep us vigilant for the possibility of danger. It is a primal and essential emotion to keep us from becoming complacent or ignoring situations where we, or someone we care about, may be harmed.

We can confuse emotions such as fear, uncertainty, apprehension, and doubt with anxiety, and it can also become habitual. If we grew up in a home that didn't feel safe to us or if we've been warned often of the consequences of failure, anxiety may have become our default emotion no matter what the situation. Even if there is no possibility of harm, we are still on high alert.

Shifting out of habitual anxiety requires that we identify an emotion that would serve us better and design a practice for strengthening it. For instance, since anxiety relates to the future, we might pick an emotion that anchors us in the present like gratitude. Or we might select an emotion like faith that also relates to the future but shifts us from an inward to an outward focus.

Instead of running from anxiety or trying to suppress it, we may find it is more useful to acknowledge that we feel anxious, check whether there is truly danger on the horizon or it is habitual anxiety at play, then shift to an emotion that serves us better and frees up our creative energy. What is your process?

Anxiety

Story: "I believe something may harm me, but I'm not sure what it might come from."

Impulse: To worry

Purpose: Warn us of possible danger even if we can't identify what the danger might be

---

Source: "The Field Guide to Emotions" by Dan Newby and Curtis Watkins

Hello Emotions!

FEAR

F ear whispers scary stories about death, cancer, failure, being judged, and other difficult experiences. Everything she murmurs sounds convincing, sounds inevitable, or has severe consequences, and sometimes this paralyzes us.

One day Fear came when I was preparing the materials for an upcoming training class.

Hello Emotions!

"How surprising to see you! What brings you here, Fear? I've taught this subject countless times. Besides, it is my favorite topic, and I long to share what I know with people. Given all of that, what could provoke my fear?" I stared at Fear in astonishment.

Fear looked me in the eye and softly said, "What if the participants in tomorrow's workshop understand your lessons but they do not apply them and as a result don't experience the transformation you hope for?"

"Then it will not be a successful class," I calmly replied.

"Then what will happen to you? Your clients will no longer trust you. There will be no more new contracts, no new chances for you to teach and share your passion for this topic. Then maybe you will have to go back to your old career, but the scariest thing is that you will not be able to live the life you are beginning to love so much."

It dawned on me that day that Fear cared deeply for me and was showing it by trying to protect me. As soon as she sensed I started valuing something, she began to panic at the sight of potential risks of losing it. She tirelessly warned me with dark visions of a day when my treasure was no longer there for me.

Looking back at all the storms that had passed through my life, I realized that loss was not as scary as waking up every day under the dark sky Fear was telling me about. Loss gives birth to a new journey and opens a new chapter with exciting and thrilling challenges. Those are the driving forces and the energy of life.

I took a deep, long breath, smiled, and answered Fear, "What you are warning me about is possible. I will just do my best, and I am ready for the worst to happen. Thank you for letting me know what I cherish the most and for giving me this great lesson so I can live a life filled with bravery."

▶ *Does Fear wake up with you every morning?*

▶ *What is she trying to warn you about?*

▶ *Are you ready for the worst to happen and do you welcome exciting challenges?*

DAN'S THOUGHTS

Fear is primal. We feel it at our core. When intense, it causes us to hide, freeze, run from, or deny what is happening. We often try to talk ourselves and others out of fear by saying things like, "There's nothing to be afraid of," "It will be okay," or "I promise I won't let anything hurt you." While our intentions are good, they are often misplaced.

Fear has such an important role in our lives. Its intensity gets our attention and it warns us about possible danger. It triggers a reaction faster than we can process it intellectually. In that guise, it keeps us safe, or at least safer. But, at times, fear keeps us from engaging with others, pursuing a dream, or trying out a new activity. It can isolate us and be a tremendous barrier to things we truly desire.

Although we may be tempted to think of fear as negative, the better question is whether the level of fear we are experiencing is appropriate for the situation. Are we overestimating the risk? Is the fear triggered because of a previous experience that cannot repeat itself? To what degree is fear keeping us safe and to what degree is it a barrier? If it is a barrier, what emotion or emotions could we access to support us moving beyond our fear?

Fear

Story: "I believe something may harm me, and I know what it is."

Impulse: To avoid perceived danger

Purpose: Help us avoid danger

Source: "The Field Guide to Emotions" by Dan Newby and Curtis Watkins

FEAR OF JUDGMENT

When the Covid pandemic began, I was deeply unsettled. I surfed YouTube in search of calming, soothing videos. A broadcast titled "Sit Still and Watch the Ups and Downs" by Thay Minh Niem, the author of the bestseller *Understanding the Heart*, immediately caught my attention. At that moment, the name of that video spoke to me.

Hello Emotions!

A few months later, a friend of mine suggested the audiobook *Old Path White Clouds* by Thay Thich Nhat Hanh with such conviction that it intrigued me. The printed version of the book was given to me about ten years ago, but just reading the first few pages put me to sleep. Out of curiosity, I downloaded the audiobook in Vietnamese.

For those who do not know about this book, it tells the life story of the Buddha on his path to enlightenment and nirvana.

The audiobook was indeed amazing thanks to the narrator's voice, which showed lots of love and admiration for Buddha. I tried listening to a few chapters and got hooked without noticing. One night while relaxing and enjoying the narrator's soothing voice, I was startled when the storyteller introduced a new chapter titled "Maintaining Equanimity During the Ups and Downs." I chuckled, thinking Thay Minh Niem must have drawn his inspiration from this chapter when naming his broadcast. After that, I listened more attentively to see what other similarities I could notice.

The story tells about the time when Buddhism became popular. More and more people throughout the kingdom accepted the Path of Awakening, which threatened other spiritual sects. They hatched a plot to harm the Buddha's reputation by killing an attractive young woman and burying her body in a grave not too far from the Buddha's hut. They carried the victim's body through the city accusing the Buddhist congregation of the murder and trying to shake people's trust. The situation this produced was abysmal, because the congregation had no evidence to the contrary, and many people's faith was severely damaged.

I paused the audiobook, enjoying my thoughts. Something exciting was emerging. It seemed that Thay Thich Nhat Hanh, who I always admired for his insights, wisdom, and intellect, was wrong. How could Thay name the chapter "Maintaining Equanimity during the Ups and Downs"? It should have been "Sit Still and Watch the Ups and Downs." After tasting this victory for a few minutes, I was startled. If I had been in a similar situation, the best I would've been able to do was "sit still," but this was Buddha. Buddha could certainly remain centered.

Struck by that realization, I sat silently for what felt like an eternity. Though I had learned how people often judge others through their own lens, this was the first time I experienced and felt its effects so clearly. I truly felt that I could never fully understand what other people might think or feel. For the first time, it dawned on me that no one could understand or see me as fully as I could. Every single person who knew me only saw part of me, meaning their judgment was never complete and accurate.

Curiosity led me to do a little experiment. I asked my friends and a few respected past clients who knew me quite well to give me three words they believed best described me. I asked them to do it quickly, within ten seconds, to ensure their words came off the top of their head and were not filtered. The results brought me a set of unique words such as "trustworthy," "peaceful," "caring," "sincere," even "cynical" and so on.

Whether it was a negative or a positive description, I understood why those friends made their assessments. It was because they had interacted with different parts of my daily work and life. Even if it was a truthful description I considered negative, I no longer worried, because I had been growing and transforming every day. Their perspective might have been correct only at the time we had met and interacted.

I am truly grateful for the profound experience I had that night while listening to the audiobook. It helped me overcome the belief that Fear usually whispered: "What people think about you defines who you are. You will never have a chance to grow and change their judgment."

▶ *How does fear of judgment keep you from doing what you would like to do?*

▶ *Has your fear of judgment ever been helpful?*

▶ *How have you been able to overcome or move past your fear of judgment?*

DAN'S THOUGHTS

Fear is an emotion that can sometimes be linked to a specific area of our lives. Jealousy can be thought of as the fear of losing a connection or relationship. We can fear rejection or losing our social standing. The reason fear is associated with these is to warn us of possible danger. Fear does not mean there "is" danger but only that there "might be, so best to pay attention."

Sometimes we have a fear of fear itself. If we notice this, it may be because we have a story or belief that we could get stuck in fear. We may be concerned that fear will become our mood. People who live in the mood of fear see a world that appears to be full of danger. Their circumstances may not be more dangerous than any other person's, but they believe the danger is real. It looks true to them.

When I coach people who are blocked by fear, I don't focus on why they feel fear. Fear exists, it is the way they see things, and for them, it is a barrier. That is often enough to know. I do always inquire if the fear is helpful or supportive in some way. I follow that by asking if they want to remain in the fear or shift it. These are essential to be sure the client doesn't interpret fear as an emotion to avoid and something that is driving the conversation.

The question that helps people move through fear is what emotion they would prefer to be in. What emotion do they think would give them the energy to do what they are hesitating to do or to take a step in the direction they want? People choose from an enormous range of emotions—inspiration, boldness, compassion, faith, enthusiasm, dignity, acceptance, and others.

In the end, they see that fear isn't even the true barrier. What is holding them back is their attention on their fear. The best strategy may be to focus on the emotion that fuels them and leave the fear to fade. Fear won't leave them. It will show up again to remind them of possible danger but will become less and less of a barrier. We do not need, and wouldn't want to, eliminate fear. Sometimes, we just need to take it out of the spotlight.

INDIGNATION

During the Covid pandemic in 2020, I signed a large contract with a corporate client to run a series of team development activities using a virtual approach. The outcomes of the first few workshops with management trainees and HR team members were great, with high energy, laughter, a lot of interaction, and questions from the audiences, which resulted in high assessment and recommendation scores.

To my and my client's HR partner's surprise, the energy dropped a few weeks later in the third and fourth workshops when the program was rolled out to senior leaders. In these seminars, some participants did their own work and refused to turn on their cameras or stayed silent. Their disengagement was contagious, impacting other participants, resulting in a mood that kept me awake at night.

The next day when I opened my laptop wondering what to write to my HR partner, Indignation arrived. He looked serious:

"Thao, all you were supposed to do was to help your clients appreciate their talents and learn to unlock their potential. But I noticed you had to pull and push very hard. The energy you spent on these last two workshops was almost double the first two. These attendees just sat there disengaged and giving bad feedback. You can't let people treat you that way. You deserve much better!"

"You are right, Indignation," I replied, "this situation has never happened before. My past clients have always been excited to uncover their talents and strengths. Many of them couldn't wait to respond or ask questions in the workshops. Here there was silence after every one of my questions, which made the atmosphere heavier with each passing minute. It seems that the participants believed that the success or failure of the program was solely my responsibility."

Indignation

I wrote an email and booked a discussion with the HR partners to share my experiences and observations and to seek help. A few minutes of chatting gave me new insight into the situation: These participants were nominated for the training by their line managers!

Somehow the word "nomination" hit me hard. "Nomination" means that while you are sitting at your desk, working nonstop to meet a dozen deadlines, suddenly out of nowhere you receive an email from your boss saying, "Congratulations! You've been nominated to attend a training course." The objectives may have been clearly stated in the email, but you were distracted by the many other things you had to think and worry about. You told yourself, "I'll read it later." "Later" never came, and the workshop date arrived. Again you told yourself, "I'll figure it out in the workshop; the trainer will tell us." But I did not review the objectives because I, the trainer, assumed that everything had been communicated and understood beforehand.

By the end of the discussion, I saw I bore the responsibility for not reiterating the training objectives and what the participants could expect. I also asked the HR partner to communicate the shared responsibility the participants had before each session started.

The results of the remaining four workshops were beyond our expectations. Quite often during the workshop, we heard a "complaint" like "Why does time fly so fast? We still have so much to share!" One director asked me and the HR manager to stay for a few minutes after the training ended. He shared his surprise about the engagement through the virtual approach and asked us to lead a similar program with his team. I also received a few emails asking how to get a coaching certificate like mine.

I have learned a precious lesson from Indignation. When I have tried my best and have worked with all my heart and soul, I deserve to be treated well. When I am not, the solution must come from better understanding the other person's pain. When someone does not treat us well, they must have their own suffering.

▶ *Have you ever confused Indignation with Anger?*

▶ *When Indignation paid you a visit, what did you do?*

▶ *By putting yourself in the shoes of others, would you like to do something differently when he visits you next time?*

DAN'S THOUGHTS

Indignation is the emotion that helps us protect our worthiness. It is the emotion that shows up when someone crosses a personal boundary. It is the emotion that allows us to defend the stand we take for ourselves.

Imagine your life without this emotion. You would have no tool to stop people from treating you disrespectfully, ignoring you, or taking advantage of you. When we lack access to dignity, we often are unable to muster up indignation. We confuse it with anger, which has a different purpose.

When I express indignation, I am not claiming I am right or that I know the truth; I am only saying that I do not permit others to treat me as I'm being treated. In reality, no one can do this for us. Others can try to protect us in various ways, but only we can set and defend our boundaries.

Indignation

Story: "I refuse to be treated in this way."

Impulse: To protect or defend myself and my identity

Purpose: Take care of myself and preserve my personal boundaries

Source: "The Field Guide to Emotions" by Dan Newby and Curtis Watkins

Hello Emotions!

ACCEPTANCE

A few months ago, the bitter melons in my garden were growing cheerfully. Dozens of vines competed to climb over the fence into the neighbor's yard. Their flowers bloomed a sparkling golden shade, but they never bore fruit. After seeing that every day I waited in vain for the melons to appear, my mother said, "I saw your brother putting pollen into his flowers, and his plants produced an abundance of melons."

Oh! If that was the secret, it was easy. Without waiting a second, I diligently picked the pollen from one flower and put it on the pistil of another. The flowers fell to the ground after being touched. I was frustrated but didn't give up. I continued to give all my plants "arranged marriages."

Many days passed with no fruit, until one morning to my immense surprise I discovered a tiny bitter melon fruit carrying a flower bud on its head. After a few days, the flower bloomed and the fruit grew. Now I understood. That flower was female and had been ready to produce fruit since birth. The flowers I dedicated time and effort to match had all been male flowers! Oh my! That "magnificent" discovery made me laugh so hard, lifting a heavy weight from my chest.

Looking around, I saw Acceptance grinning mischievously. He said, "Now I guess you have finally accepted the laws of nature, haven't you?" I chuckled. "Yes," I replied, "I just didn't know that was what I needed to do. Only a fool would go against such obvious laws of nature."

In my younger years, Acceptance was not included in my dictionary of emotions. I used to believe Acceptance meant giving up too early and easily. Since I began to practice observing the way life works, I have come to realize that Acceptance helps me save energy and avoid pointless battles, hence giving me more time for Peace and Fulfillment.

Acceptance

When I learned to accept that I would never reach perfection, I began to allow myself to make mistakes without being haunted by self-criticism. I also become more accepting of others' mistakes without the temptation to criticize them.

When I learned to accept the limitations of my physical health, I stopped moaning and regretting the passing of my youth. Instead, I immediately changed my eating habits and adjusted my working schedule so that I could work and live with greater well-being.

When I learned to accept that every person filters the world through their unique lens, I gradually let go of the temptation of assessing right or wrong and gained more confidence in sharing my thoughts. After all, often right and wrong are assessments, aren't they?

When I learned to accept that I can't force others to change their behaviors or habits to please me, I began to look inside myself to understand what prevents me from being able to accept them as they are. Now, searching for deep insights into myself and accepting others as they are is my strategy to continue living in peace.

When I learned to accept the impermanence of life, I stopped letting my emotions run too high when I am at the peak of glory. I know that soon everything may begin going downhill at full speed, catching me off guard if I am not mindful. I also do not feel resentful when I experience unexpected events; instead, I crawl into my shell, enjoy the day leisurely, and wait for the storm to pass.

Acceptance has brought peace and serenity to my daily life.

What about you? In which aspects of your life could you invite greater Acceptance? Is there anything you need to change so Acceptance can visit you more often?

- ▶ *Do you think of Acceptance as surrender or giving up?*
- ▶ *Have you ever tried declaring Acceptance rather than waiting for it to show up?*
- ▶ *What do you need to accept today that would bring more ease to your life?*

DAN'S THOUGHTS

In my experience, few emotions are as misunderstood as acceptance. Many people have learned an interpretation that includes agreeing, endorsing, or surrendering. This is unfortunate because it robs acceptance of much of its potential.

Acceptance means nothing more than "receiving what is offered." In other words, we are acknowledging "what is." We are at peace. It doesn't mean we like the way things are or that we would have chosen for them to be this way, but we are not resisting them. Acceptance can be summed up in the statement "It is so."

When someone says, "I accept that my son doesn't want to attend university, but ..." we know that they are not in acceptance. Tolerance, perhaps, but not acceptance.

Acceptance

At times we may struggle to accept a situation that is painful or that was not of our choosing and can be held back by the belief that we need to wait for acceptance to show up. It can and does, but we also have the ability to declare acceptance. We can declare we will never understand why someone ended a relationship with us, but we will not fight it any longer. We may struggle to understand why a friend passed away at a young age, but we can declare our acceptance that it is so and perhaps there is not an answer.

Sometimes we tell ourselves we "should" be able to accept a situation or person's unpleasant behavior. I believe that acceptance must be freely chosen. There are things in life that we may choose not to accept. That is up to us. The only thing we should remember is that as long as we are not in acceptance, we will put energy into changing the situation or wishing it would change. Sometimes that is perfect, but if our desire is inner peace, it is worth reflecting on.

Acceptance

Story: "It is so even though I may not agree, endorse, or like it."

Impulse: To be at peace with what is

Purpose: Help us align with reality

Source: "The Field Guide to Emotions" by Dan Newby and Curtis Watkins

Hello Emotions!

NOSTALGIA

Nostalgia has a romantic name and appears in the guise of a sweet emotion. When I first heard his name, I thought he was only good at torturing people who had been in love. I never thought that his gentleness could shake the career prospects of so many people. The more success and glorious feats one has achieved, the more suffering one may experience because of Nostalgia. Surprised?

Hello Emotions!

Nostalgia has just one trick: to remind us of our sweet memories!

When I decided to quit my job and say goodbye to my previous life to pursue coaching as my profession, my determination was limitless. No matter what my friends and colleagues suggested or advised, I ignored them. I longed to resign as soon as possible to begin living my purpose. But, after I had traveled this new road for some time and my old life was a tiny dot on the horizon, my heart still melted every time Nostalgia visited.

Nostalgia didn't say much. Once in a while he only reminded me of something like: "Hey, look at that Llaollao frozen yogurt store. Remember the weekends you hung out there with friends and enjoyed their company?" or "Do you see the rain trees over there? Remember the time you strolled along the street under their huge shady foliage in Singapore?" or "Your former colleagues have just posted their photos on Facebook. You used to enjoy endless chitchat with them there, remember?"

That was all that was needed to cause my heart to ache. I sat in silence for hours, searching through photos from the past posted on my Instagram account. Every place I looked was full of beautiful memories. When my heart became heavy, Sadness raised her voice, "It looks like you have lost something very important," she said, and Regret chimed in with "Do you think it was wise to change your life so radically?"

Those who have ventured to launch a start-up, change careers, move to a new company, rotate to a new position, or relocate to another country understand that no opportunity comes only with advantages. These changes are always accompanied by challenges from people (new boss, new team members, new business partners, new clients), a new culture, knowledge, skills, and things we don't anticipate. When we face obstacles or discomfort, Nostalgia may capture and immobilize us.

I did not notice the presence of Nostalgia at the beginning of my coaching journey and he didn't appear for quite a while. But, one morning after Covid restrictions were lifted, I put on my sneakers and went jogging in my sparsely populated neighborhood. It was a route that I hadn't taken for almost a year. That day there was something strange about the route. After the night's rain, the trees were deeply green and freshly scented. I passed a row of small, beautiful adolescent tamarind trees with countless tiny leaves forming clusters of foliage. From afar they looked like dainty girls with floating curly hair, strangely arrogant.

Surprise patted my shoulder, "Wow! Those tamarind trees are stunning! They must have been planted lately. Where are the rain trees, the most stunning trees on earth?" "Hmmm … where are my dear rain trees?" I asked myself. Searching, I found that the rain trees were still there next to their new neighboring tamarind trees. But the rain trees seemed so odd today. They were … normal. I had to run closer to take a careful look. They were still my enchanting rain trees, always showing up in Nostalgia's story, making me miss Singapore deeply. They looked the same as in a photo I took with my phone a year earlier when I first discovered them in this neighborhood.

Hello Emotions!

I was shocked. I suddenly realized that for many years I had never looked at the rain trees through a normal lens. They were always contemplated with Nostalgia (reminiscing about the beautiful days in the country I loved), Pride (being an employee at a famous multinational company), and a bit of Arrogance.

The normal look of the rain trees that day reminded me that the old days were not all just good memories and that the stories Nostalgia whispered in my ear day after day were only half of the picture. I laughed hard at this, because I realized I had been fooled by Nostalgia for so many months. On the day of parting, I turned to Nostalgia: "I know I had many beautiful memories, but now they have become my past. Today I am determined to create a new chapter with lots of fond memories. Goodbye!"

On my coaching journey, I was surprised to run into Nostalgia again when I contemplated the challenges faced by many of my respected clients. It seems the more they have achieved, the more they tend to suffer from Nostalgia's trick. It keeps them stuck with the question, "Did I make the right choice?" Even worse, it sometimes traps them in dissatisfaction with their current achievements and makes the challenges ahead even more intimidating.

▶ *Does Nostalgia visit you often?*
▶ *What memories does he bring you?*
▶ *Are you ready to let go of the past and start creating the future starting today?*

DAN'S THOUGHTS

As Thao has so sweetly illustrated, nostalgia allows us to recall times and experiences that we enjoyed. We fondly remember people we were with and things we achieved. We may feel pulled back to those times or attempt to re-create them in the present.

Nostalgia, though, can also help us plan our future. It connects us with things we enjoyed, people we appreciated, and places we were happy. Those can be used as archetypes or models for the future we create. If we are nostalgic for a place, we might ask ourselves, "What were the characteristics of that place that I enjoyed so much?" The same with people, experiences, challenges, successes, food, and every other part of life.

Nostalgia helps us appreciate the good things from our past and is also a wonderful tool to help us design a future that will be satisfying and enjoyable.

Nostalgia

Story: "The past was better than the present, and I wish I could go back."

Impulse: To yearn for the past

Purpose: Show us how good life can be from previous experiences

Source: "The Field Guide to Emotions" by Dan Newby and Curtis Watkins

GRATITUDE

Do you believe that the way we use language has the power to change the emotions we feel and even our quality of life?

Imagine this situation. Out of the blue, your boss announces a promotion much earlier than you expected, an offer to relocate to a country where you always dreamed of living, or your team exceeds your company's annual sales target thanks to favorable external factors. What would you think? "I am lucky" or "I am grateful"?

"I am lucky" was always the first and only thought to emerge in my brain when I was in similar situations. It makes sense, doesn't it? Those achievements were never in my plan, coming to me out of nowhere and beyond my expectations. What to call it if not good luck?

A few years ago, when I had acquired an understanding of emotions, I began to identify, name, and "chat" with them as emotional friends. I realized that my favorite motto "I'm lucky" always invited Anxiety to come and celebrate in these joyful moments. Immediately afterward, Joy would shout, "Oh my,

I can't believe I got promoted so soon. I am so lucky!" Anxiety then whispered, "It's just good luck, there's nothing to be so happy about … no one is lucky for their entire life … you know nothing is permanent; bad luck always comes after good luck…" When Anxiety lectured me, Joy disappeared, leaving me alone with worry.

I have completely forgotten the moment that the sentence "I am grateful" got lodged in my stubborn head. But, for me, that simple three-word sentence works like a charm, attracting numerous pleasant emotions to join me at that moment: Gratitude, Peace, Satisfaction, Fulfillment, Pride, Happiness, and Joy.

When I tell myself "I'm grateful," Anxiety stops because what I have received is not random. It has been given to me, and I believe I will be granted many more unexpected gifts if I continue to dedicate myself to serving other people. "I am grateful" gives me a sense of self-control, a feeling that I can create many good things for myself rather than sitting around waiting for good luck.

In the past, when something went wrong, Anger, Resentment, Frustration, Disappointment, or Hate would always "be there for me." Since the day I have embraced the mantra "I'm grateful," they've never come to visit. Instead, the visitors are Gratitude (I am protected), Satisfaction (I have learned a meaningful lesson), and Pride (I survive and I am stronger).

When I got stuck in traffic on a busy afternoon, Gratitude showed me that if I had gotten home a little earlier, I would have been caught in a bad thunderstorm. When my proposal for a prospect was declined, Gratitude showed up a short time later and I felt relief because the next and bigger opportunity would have been lost if I had committed to the previous client. Then just last month, Gratitude helped me appreciate a severe sore throat and fever that lasted three weeks. During that time I couldn't meet up with anyone, so I had me-time to relax and read a few precious books. If I had kept working as hard as I typically would during the busyness at the end of the year, I would not have gotten this valuable knowledge for my personal development growth.

So, I have become addicted to Gratitude without noticing. I start my day with Gratitude, telling her I am grateful for feeling healthy every morning when I wake up, for having fresh air to breathe, enough food for each mealtime, and the time to listen to the sparrows chirping or contemplate my green vegetables. My energy seems to be boosted whenever Gratitude is around. And by the end of the day when I tell Gratitude how fulfilled and satisfied I am with my life, a good sleep comes much more easily, preparing me for another fresh morning.

The mantra "I'm grateful" has helped me eliminate the notion of good and bad luck and enjoy my work and life every day. How about you?

▶ *Which emotional friends are with you when you say "I am lucky"?*

▶ *Which emotional companions are with you when you say "I am grateful"?*

▶ *What is the role of Gratitude in your life? And what will you do from today to invite Gratitude to your "house" more often?*

DAN'S THOUGHTS

The English word gratitude comes from the Latin root *gratis,* meaning "for free." This tells us a lot about the emotion. When we reflect on our life, we may realize that many of the best things we've experienced arrived as gifts. They may not be things we deserve or even earned, but they came to us nonetheless.

Gratitude

Gratitude is different from thanks. Thankfulness shows up when we are satisfied with an exchange. I purchase some fruit, pay the store clerk, and say "thank you." It can also be an expression of appreciation for a service another has performed. Gratitude is the acknowledgment that life itself is a gift.

When gratitude is not a familiar emotion, it may seem some-what mysterious. How can one feel gratitude for the bad things that happen to us? Isn't that naïveté or denial? When gratitude is easily accessible, we can ask ourselves, "What possible benefit might this experience have for me?" From that question, we will find the gift.

At one time I lived in the mood of entitlement. I believed that "the world owed me" certain things in terms of my status, level of income, size of my house, a sports car, type of relationship. This expectation made me miserable and resentful because "the world was not doing its part." I decided that the mood I wanted to live in was gratitude. Daily I reflected on the gifts I received, I intervened in my thoughts when they drifted toward entitlement, and I challenged myself to find the benefit in all that happened. Over time my mood of entitlement shifted to a by-default mood of gratitude.

Entitlement still shows up, of course, but I know now that I don't have to believe what it is saying. I am not obligated to go down the path that leads to dissatisfaction and resentment. I can choose to refocus on gratitude, which brings peace. It is a choice we all have.

Gratitude

Story: "Life and everything that is a part of it is a gift."

Impulse: To appreciate all that we have received and do receive each day

Purpose: Make us realize that life itself is a gift and not something we have earned

Source: "The Field Guide to Emotions" by Dan Newby and Curtis Watkins

SADNESS

Sadness is a deep, gentle, and understanding friend. We can sit next to each other by the window contemplating the moon and stars, without needing to speak. Every time Sadness comes, my body feels comfortably heavy. That is when I allow myself to temporarily forget my ambitious goals and put aside all my pending projects to be with Sadness.

Sadness knows I enjoy those relaxing moments with her. Yet she rarely visits, and when she does, she leaves quickly after giving a clear answer to my question, "Hey, tell me what important thing I have lost." But once Sadness came and sat quietly without saying even a single word.

That morning I had coffee and a chat with a friend. Like me, he had left the corporate world and had been pursuing coaching as a profession for some time. He proposed that we collaborate and asked, "What do you think?" My heart skipped a beat. Oh! Finally, this day had come. I no longer had to be alone on this journey, I thought. Excited, we talked nonstop about our plans. I left the meeting full of Joy grinning from ear to ear.

When I got home at noon, Sadness was sitting on the front porch. Surprised, I asked: "Hello, my friend. Did you come on the wrong day? I'm ecstatic today. Joy came home with me. See?" Sadness was silent. That night I was restless and could not sleep. Sadness sat next to me. I don't know what she cooked and ate for dinner, but during the night she doubled in size. I slept superficially and had many dreams.

When I awoke in the morning, the first thing I noticed missing was freedom. I had thought my freedom was unlimited compared to the days I worked in an office. It seemed that I must be wrong. I had already lost the freedom that money could buy. Why did this feeling come just now? Hadn't I been away from my old life for a long time and gotten used to my new humble lifestyle?

It turned out that deep down I was holding onto a hope that one day I would have everything I once had—the freedom to travel anywhere at any time I wished, staying in luxurious resorts, shopping without having to remember the price of every item ...

During yesterday's coffee, for the first time, I heard stories about the journeys of those who had stepped into the coaching territory years before me, about the lives of those who were pursuing the same path. That was when I came to realize I had forever lost the freedom that I once had and was proud of!

For the first time, I no longer hated the previous version of me, the aggressive and demanding me, with only business results as my focus. If I had brought the current version of me into my prior world, I would not have survived.

For the first time, I could explain why from time to time I missed those past moments so badly. It was not because I missed the old me, but because I had happy, free, and memorable moments in that world. For the first time, I appreciated both the past and the present.

For the first time, I loved both worlds—the one I had left and the one I had been pursuing. Living in either world was simply a choice. Each had its fun and challenges. The choice was up to each person.

And I chose to continue taking the path less traveled, as I had fallen in love with my life purpose and my modest life. Sadness gently looked at me and smiled. She slowly shrank and disappeared, knowing I was now ready to let go of something I once treasured.

▶ *Is Sadness often with you?*

▶ *Did you lose something you cared about deeply?*

▶ *Are you ready to let it go, or what will you do to re-create it?*

DAN'S THOUGHTS

How often do you allow yourself to experience sadness? How often do you make space for those around you to experience it? Perhaps not much. Sadness has long been on the list of emotions we consider inherently negative, and our first reaction is often to chase it away.

We "get busy" doing something important, we divert our attention through entertainment, or we try to talk ourselves out of our sadness. We try to cheer up those around us, telling them, "There is nothing to be sad about," as if we knew. The unfortunate part of these well-intentioned actions is that we miss what is so important about our sadness, what it is pointing to.

Sadness

Sadness arrives to inform us that we have lost something we care about. Just caring about someone isn't enough to provoke sadness. Just losing something isn't enough. It is always a combination of the two. It need not be something material, a thing or person, but can also be immaterial. We may feel sadness when we lose our innocence or notice the strength of our youth diminishing.

And sadness is not always about the past. We can use it as a tool to test what and who we care about. If we imagine someone no longer being in our lives, the level of sadness we feel will reflect the degree to which we care about that person. The same is true for an object, role at work, or living situation. So running away from sadness or ignoring what it is trying to show us restricts our understanding of what and who we truly care about.

Sadness

Story: "I've lost something I care about."

Impulse: To withdraw and grieve

Purpose: Show us what is important to us

Source: "The Field Guide to Emotions" by Dan Newby and Curtis Watkins

Hello Emotions!

ADVENTUROUSNESS

Adventurousness is the instigator of any wild trick he can invent. He simply cannot live without heart-stopping experiences.

One Monday, Adventurousness came knocking loudly at my door. Seeing that I was staring at my laptop, he rushed in, pulled me up, and urged me to pack my suitcase with all the essentials for a trip. When I asked where he wanted to go, he shrugged: "Anywhere is fine as long as it is not here."

Hello Emotions!

Given that it was Monday, I had many deadlines to prepare for during the week. Besides, all my friends were occupied, so they couldn't accompany me. I would have to travel alone with Adventurousness this time. It looked like he had set a trap for me. But where to go? It was a hectic time of the year with my regular coaching appointments, designing new training courses, and the preparation of proposals I had promised my business partners. Well, I thought, let's take a short trip to Dalat then, the attraction closest to my hometown.

After twenty minutes, the reservations were made. At noon we were both seated on a bus and were warmly welcomed by an elderly couple to their homey mansion at midnight. In the morning when I woke up, I lay in bed and took in the pleasantly strange feeling of this new place. Outside the window of my cozy room, the sun was beaming brightly, the wind joyfully teasing leaves on the trees, and far away a road was meandering over the hills that surround serene Lake Tuyen Lam.

Adventurousness couldn't hold his excitement anymore:

"That hilly road is breathtaking! Please quit your timid habit of exploring a new place by taxi. This time let's rent a motor-bike. It is much more fun!"

In a flash, the two of us were driving up the hill. On one side were pine trees, on the other was the beautiful and mesmerizing Lake Tuyen Lam. In the peaceful stillness, I heard a group of "people" shouting:

Adventurousness

Adventurousness: "The wind is so cold. It's like going on a winter vacation."

Someone: "We only wore a thin jacket. We'll die if we catch a cold."

Adventurousness: "The street is empty. Driving here is so liberating!"

Someone: "Control your speed! We are not used to this new motorbike."

Adventurousness: "Oh my! The lake is so beautiful! My heart is melting."

Someone: "Watch the road! Watch the road! What if a big car comes around the bend from below?"

Adventurousness: "Look at that picturesque spot! Let's shoot a few photos there."

Someone: "That place is scarily empty. Don't stop, don't stop!"

"Who are those absurd people I keep hearing?" I wondered. Looking back, I saw Fear and Anxiety hugging Adventurousness tightly. Their faces were pale.

The next morning I got up and continued driving down the road that made my heart melt yesterday. Everything was strangely quiet. Adventurousness had been missing since early morning. Anxiety and Fear were also hiding. Traveling for a while, I heard someone whisper:

"Boring! let's go home!"

Looking over, I saw Boredom was sitting next to me cross-legged. I was surprised: "Wow, so soon? It's only been two days."

He shrugged. "Yesterday you traveled back and forth on this route several times. At first, it was breathtaking. Now you're racing so fast that Fear can't even catch you. There aren't any interesting challenges left."

For the first time, I was surprised to realize the up-and-down cycle of my career path over the past fifteen years. It always started with Adventurousness, who urged me to embark on a new journey. Excitement and Passion visited me for the first few days, then Anxiety and Fear followed me to the office every day due to the many challenges, responsibilities, and expectations. After a few years, when I had gained a solid foothold in the field and was trusted by many people, Boredom always showed up asking to stay with me. Could it be that at the age of 80, with gray hair, looking back over the whole journey, my memories would only be moments with Anxiety, Fear, and Boredom?

That day was a big day in my life, and I made a bold declaration:

"Anxiety and Fear, thank you both for always letting me know the potential risks that await. But starting from today, you definitely can't stay at my house. As for Boredom, I won't spend time hanging out with you anymore. Every time you come, I know it's time to start a new journey with Adventurousness."

That was the journey in which Adventurousness helped me uncover new insights into my career path.

▶ *When was the last time Adventurousness asked you to do something heart-stopping?*

▶ *What did you learn from that experience?*

▶ *What stands in the way of releasing your Adventurousness?*

DAN'S THOUGHTS

Routines, habits, predictability, steadiness are elements of stability. Stability is something we all need and that we sometimes try to achieve through control. However, when these characteristics begin to dominate your way of living, you may begin to feel the need to break out, change, or explore. When that happens, adventurousness may be the emotion you are looking for.

When we begin a journey, we never know what we'll encounter. We can anticipate that there will be exciting moments, discoveries, challenges, discomfort, and surprises. Adventurousness allows us to roll all these into one bundle. We know there will be difficult moments, but believe they will be worth whatever pain they cause.

Adventure means to "wander, travel, seek" and "to take a chance." When we begin an adventure we give up what is familiar to experience something new. Although we associate adventure with exploring new places, it can just as readily apply to new thoughts, practicing new crafts or arts, cooking, or relationships. It does not need to be material or physical.

When was the last time you deliberately gave your imagination free rein to wander, explore, and discover? When did you choose to step out of your known world and comfort zone to experience something new, different, and even a bit exotic? You can do this any day you choose by connecting with adventurousness and unleashing its power.

Adventurousness

Story: "I'm ready for a new experience."

Impulse: To explore

Purpose: Get us exploring in the world

Source: "The Field Guide to Emotions" by Dan Newby and Curtis Watkins

LONELINESS

Loneliness has chubby cheeks and a big appetite. Monopolizing our relationship is his unique trick. He often whispers: "Friends are not fun. All of them are boring. You and I are enough."

Loneliness spoils his friends by taking them shopping, traveling, eating out, and encouraging them to do whatever they yearn for. He can sit with you for hours, eating from one dish or the other without getting bored.

Loneliness has a twin brother named Lonesomeness, who goes by the nickname "Solitude." If Loneliness makes you feel empty and lacking something you cannot describe, Lonesomeness makes you feel satisfied without anyone else around. Loneliness's favorite saying is "I'm alone and something is missing," while Lonesomeness loves his mantra "I am alone, yet I feel complete."

When I first started my journey into the world of coaching and psychology, I felt like a fish in water. Everything was so fascinating. I loved each piece of new knowledge and enjoyed every awakening. What I liked the most was the ability to look deep inside, into every nook and cranny, to get a better understanding of myself. They gave me an explanation for the many burning questions that had lingered for years and helped me make countless extremely satisfying decisions without needing to consult anyone.

I became obsessive about being alone to contemplate, ponder, and uncover the insights, wisdom, and solutions to all my questions and problems. Then I became too lazy to meet friends. I heard someone saying: "From now on, it is unnecessary to meet friends anymore. They always talk about boring and shallow topics. Your thoughts are so deep and insightful. No one can understand you as you do. Going out only wastes time and energy. It is more fun and comfortable at home."

"Whose voice is that?" I wondered, "It is probably Lonesomeness. I am not lonely. I am busy at work, meeting clients and business partners every day, chitchatting, and gossiping with my closest friends around the world at any time I want. I definitely cannot be living with Loneliness."

One day I began to fear everything—fear of illness, fear of failure, even fear of death—without understanding what was happening. One evening I could not stand the fears anymore, so I called a friend who had been pursuing a PhD in Pharmacy to have a chat about what disease I might have. After a casual catch-up with her for about thirty minutes, all my Fears disappeared. The feeling of being connected, heard, and understood was indescribable and magical. Saying goodbye to my friend, I heard someone calling me from the kitchen. "Hey, Thao, it is time for our supper. I've ordered your favorite takeout pizza. Come quick!" My goodness! I had invited Loneliness into my home, mistaking him for Lonesomeness. Sure enough, it was him. His cheeks were so chubby and he urged me to eat pizza every day.

No need to wait any longer! I made plans to see my old close friends again for coffee, lunch, and shopping together. Meeting each other, we talked about our old sweet memories, made jokes, and helped each other in our daily lives. I felt warm being connected with my friends after such a long time, even though I could not share what I had learned and how I had been enlightened on my journey so far. To fill in what was missing, I made new connections, created new groups composed of new friends, such as my Mindfulness Lovers group. Although we were all new to each other, we shared the same passions and interests. Every day we practiced and encouraged each other to become better versions of ourselves. I now feel fulfilled and solid inside out.

I learned a great lesson. Maybe there doesn't exist someone who can fully understand me. Maybe the friend I need the most will not be with me at a critical time. But it isn't necessary to feel disappointed or pursue a self-contained way of life. It is a great opportunity to open the door wide and welcome new friends who share my new focus. If one person cannot understand me in this aspect, someone else will. In an emergency, if one friend cannot come to rescue me, there will be another. I felt released and relieved by the last thought. It lifts a heavy burden off my shoulders in case I cannot be with my friends when they are in need.

- ▶ *Is Loneliness a frequent visitor?*
- ▶ *What is he saying that you are missing?*
- ▶ *What will you do to fill yourself up?*

DAN'S THOUGHTS

Sometimes it is difficult to find the word that describes exactly what we are feeling. That is to be expected, of course, because we are naming something that we cannot see and are always interpreting. Sometimes it is easier to describe the conditions we are experiencing and give that meaning to the name.

Loneliness

There is an emotion we feel when we are by ourselves and have the sense that something or someone is missing. Then there is the emotion we experience when we are by ourselves and it seems perfect. I call those loneliness and lonesomeness or solitude, although you might have other names for them.

When we are alone and there is nothing missing, we feel complete and are content. It is something to revel in and enjoy. There is a sense of unity with the universe in these moments, and we want for nothing. This is not usually an emotion we want to shift or move away from.

The emotion we feel when we are by ourselves and feel something is missing, loneliness, can be a difficult and distressing experience. Many people suffer from loneliness not just when alone, but even when they are with others. They feel disconnected, unseen, and unimportant.

I used to experience loneliness profoundly and often. I grew up always being "the new kid on the block" and rarely lived in one place for more than a year. Out of that experience, I began to believe I was alone in the world and put tremendous effort into trying to connect with others so I could rid myself of the feeling.

One day I realized that from the moment of my birth until the moment I die, being alone is a truth in the material sense. I was separate physically from other people, so feeling separate made sense. It was, after all, true. Once I accepted that I was separate and every moment of connection was a gift, I began to understand loneliness differently. I no longer tried to chase it away or avoid it and began seeing it as my natural state. Being alone didn't need to cause suffering. I began to appreciate what

I now call lonesomeness or solitude and enjoy my own company. The peace this has brought me is indescribable. I'm alone and it is fine.

Loneliness can also stem from the lack of recognition that we are an integral part of the universe. In that sense, we are never alone. It is impossible. When we feel alone, we can search for a connection with the world around us through wonder, awe, faith, or exuberance. Being connected with nature, God, the prime mover, or whatever concept we have of what is "beyond human" can help us see that we are always being held by a force greater than ourselves.

Loneliness

Story: "I am alone and something is missing."

Impulse: To seek others for company

Purpose: Urge us to seek out others to complete our sense of self

Lonesomeness (or solitude)

Story: "I am alone, yet I feel complete."

Impulse: To enjoy time with myself

Purpose: To help us appreciate the richness of time alone

Sources:
"The Field Guide to Emotions" by Dan Newby and Curtis Watkins
"The Unopened Gift" by Dan Newby and Lucy Núñez

GUILT

Guilt's secret wish is to become a stern rule enforcer one day. Whenever he sees me doing something wrong, there is no way I can escape his punishment. The first thing he tells me is, "By doing that, you broke your own standards."

I remember once that it was very cold a few days before the Lunar New Year. Among countless delicious dishes cooked in my hometown to celebrate, I craved the Indian mushroom masala curry with garlic naan bread. I skipped my snack in the afternoon to save my appetite for the special dinner that was to come. With my stomach growling, an hour waiting for the food delivery seemed like an eternity. Finally, it came. Excitedly, I opened the food box and couldn't wait to dip the first piece of naan bread into the curry I love so much. Then I noticed something wrong. "What is this? Why is there mutton in my dish?"

I had a flashback to my four years of working and living in Singapore. I ate mutton masala for lunch every day without getting bored and learned that it was one of the signature dishes of many Indian restaurants. I suspected that the restaurant owner, wanting to please his customers, secretly upgraded my mushroom order to mutton curry, hoping it would be a pleasant surprise. But now my stomach was rumbling and I couldn't touch it.

I checked my order again. It said mushroom masala. Anger urged me to pick up the phone and call to complain.

"Hello. My order just came and is incorrect. I ordered mushroom masala, so I don't understand why there is mutton in my curry."

"Yes, I know, but the mutton curry is more expensive and we thought ..."

"But how can I eat it? I am a vegetarian."

There followed several seconds of stunned silence.

Guilt

"I'm sorry," she said, "the chef cooked … I told him …"

"I understand. It's okay," I said, and ended the conversation. A few seconds later, my phone rang.

"Please give me your address to deliver the mushroom curry, we are so sorry …"

"It's okay, you don't have to make another dish for me," I said, and hung up the phone.

That was it, and Guilt tormented me the entire evening. Guilt began chastising me incessantly. "You ordered food from them a second time; they noticed that you like their food and offered more. It was their treat. You couldn't wait to calm down and text them, but had to call and complain! Now the manager and the chef are probably having a shouting match."

"So, tell me what standard you believe I have broken," I said.

He replied, "You committed to stop creating bad energy for people around you, and you broke that commitment."

"Well … I broke it this time because I was so hungry," I said, defending myself. "But I accept that I didn't live up to the standard I have set for myself in this particular case. Next time I'll wait for the anger to subside before complaining."

Guilt noted down something in his notebook and went away. My heart was lighter. That occurred a few months ago. Guilt only stayed with me for a few hours. In the past, he lingered for much longer, sometimes for a whole week, and frequently brought up old stories to lecture me about.

95

Guilt also visits my clients quite often. In a few special cases, Guilt had followed them for years, continually accusing them of past mistakes. Their release from Guilt begins when they review the standards they have set for themselves and take action based on them. Guilt then dissipates.

Quite often the standards we set for ourselves are close to perfection, such as never making others sad, being obligated to help others in any situation, or never saying anything silly, without realizing that we can never achieve and maintain that level. Each of us is on a path of self-development. Getting one step closer each day is already great progress.

▶ *Has Guilt been following you around lately?*
▶ *Which of your standards does he believe you have broken? Where did that standard come from?*
▶ *Is it a standard you choose to keep or will you revise it to let go of Guilt?*

DAN'S THOUGHTS

Do you see guilt as a beautiful emotion? Probably not. Most of us don't, but there is an aspect of guilt that is truly a gift. That awful sensation we feel when guilt shows up is a signal that something is out of alignment. It is telling us that we are not honoring our values, not meeting a standard we believe in, or are not behaving according to the norms we have committed to.

Why is that beautiful? Because it urges us to take a look. Guilt's job is to keep us in alignment with our values. It is like an attentive dog that guides a wayward sheep back to the flock. Sometimes it feels as if it is barking at us or nipping at our heels, but that is the duty it has been assigned. If it didn't feel terrible, we would ignore it and continue to stray from the path we profess to believe in.

When we feel guilt, we often look for ways to punish ourselves for our transgression. We call ourselves stupid or deny ourselves pleasure in some way. That shows we take our breach seriously, but often it is unnecessary. We could instead acknowledge that we acted out of alignment with our values, then feel appreciation that our guilt helped us confirm who we want to be and how we want to live.

Guilt

Story: "In doing that, I broke my own standards."

Impulse: To blame and punish myself

Purpose: Take care of our private identity

Source: "The Field Guide to Emotions" by Dan Newby and Curtis Watkins

Hello Emotions!

PEACE

Peace has the beaming smile of the morning sun. His eyes are as clear as dewdrops lying on mustard greens. When I sit next to Peace, all fatigue and stress dissipate. Maybe that's why Peace is permanently on the wish list of many people, including me.

Hello Emotions!

I do not know how other people pursue Peace. I, at least the version of me many years ago, was determined to buy Peace. At any cost. I believed that if I achieved the position of my dreams, lived in foreign countries making others envious, worked in prestigious companies, and owned a luxurious apartment, I could exchange it for Peace.

Peace could be bought. Really! Peace, smiling contentedly seeped into my dream every time I achieved an important milestone. Peace lay down, enjoying the sound of waves lapping against the rocks at an exotic resort. Peace sat quietly with me, watching the sunrise in some faraway land that not everyone could set foot in.

It had been a long time since I stopped chasing Peace, not because I did not need him, but because I could not afford him. I did not have the resources to buy Peace anymore. Until one day, my stomach went on strike, refused to work, couldn't digest anything I ate, and then surreptitiously tried to push the food back out. I was tired. I missed Peace so much.

It was a rainy afternoon. I sat on the sofa, enduring my rebellious stomach. Outside it was pouring rain. The foliage of the sesame fortune tree was swaying in the wind. The rain pattered and danced on the leaves, then rushed down to the ground. I sat, breathed deeply, and felt my troublesome stomach rise and fall. I smiled watching the swaying of the trees and leaves, listening to the sound of the wind and rain, taking in the smell of the earth, of the freshly washed plants, of the cool breath of early summer, and my stomach became calm. I felt relieved and warm and noticed Peace was at my side. He had been with me for a while without my noticing.

It dawned on me that it is unnecessary to chase after money, status, power, or wealth to trade for Peace. Peace can be created at any moment wherever I want. Peace is present with me whenever I put aside the hustle and bustle of work to slow down and notice the fresh morning air, the sparrows calling each other to wake up and search for bugs or a few grains of rice. Peace comes when I see the vegetables in my garden stretching toward the smiling sun or hear the sound of children laughing in the neighborhood. He visits when I hear the rain falling on the tin roof of my storage shed, breathe in the smell of wet soil, or simply enjoy each gentle breath during meditation.

- ▶ *Are you in search of Peace?*
- ▶ *Will you try to "buy" Peace?*
  OR
- ▶ *Will you create Peace for yourself?*

DAN'S THOUGHTS

There is a curious thing about the way we think about certain emotions. Sometimes we imagine they are a "thing." When we picture them this way, we can fall into the belief that we can pursue and capture them or create them. Some emotions can more easily be experienced by giving up this idea. The emotion of peace is one of these.

Peace is formally defined as "freedom from disturbance" or "the absence of war." So it isn't a thing, but rather the lack of a thing. When we are able to remove disturbances from our environment and awareness or reach a state where we have no sense of threat or danger, we may discover we feel peace.

Peace shows up in meditation, prayer, nature, in a moment when we are absorbed watching raindrops create patterns on a pond. We can experience it sitting by the ocean captivated by the rhythm of waves washing up on the beach. Watching a loved one sleep, a sunrise, or listening to a certain piece of music.

Where do you make space in your life for peace to manifest? When do you pause and set aside the dozens of other emotions you experience each day to create the possibility of peace? How could you choose peace? Like most emotions, it is always available to us if we are present to the possibility.

Peace

Story: "All is well."

Impulse: To rest

Purpose: To allow rest without concern

Source: "The Field Guide to Emotions" by Dan Newby and Curtis Watkins

ENVY

Envy has a stern look. She is rarely satisfied with what she has, always yearning for what others have. Her best friend is Hate. They sometimes invite Resentment to join them and form a gang.

One bright morning Envy knocked on my door, shouting: "Thao, do you know what? There are new classes teaching EQ and they are attracting many students. And, they are charging twice as much as you! Go to Facebook and see for yourself."

Hate chimed in: "I can't stand those people! Their content is nothing new. They must be tricking people or playing unethical games to attract their audiences."

Resentment came to sit beside me: "Life is unfair. You have been working so hard and are getting nothing!"

After listening to the three of them carping for a while, my energy level quickly dropped to zero. All excitement and enthusiasm to start the day was gone.

But what was I truly envious of? I wanted to share my knowledge with as many people as possible, but for what? Material gain or fame? No! I believed that money and fame find their way to those who deserve it. Deep down, I wanted to live a useful life, to help as many people as possible enjoy more peaceful moments in their lives.

To become a facilitator, I had to search for a teacher I respected, and it wasn't an easy journey. There were countless people with world-class degrees and reputations, but I only put my trust in a few people. What attracts me is not just the course content, but my teachers' charisma, character qualities, and contribution to society. I spent lots of time reading their articles, blogs, and books before registering for their training program. Rarely did I choose a teacher because of their advertising.

People who could open so many classes must have put enormous effort into their personal development and contributed greatly to society to gain trust from their participants. It was completely fair and deserved. What I needed to do right now and in the future was to continue working on myself and contribute more to society. The trust of my clients and students would be the most powerful certification of what I would achieve on this journey.

I thanked Envy, Hate, and Resentment for offering me another valuable lesson. It was one that boosted my energy to continue my journey.

▶ *Has Envy ever visited you?*

▶ *What is it that she says you are yearning for?*

▶ *Have you got it yet? If not, what will you do from today to achieve what you want?*

DAN'S THOUGHTS

There are many characteristics or facets of emotions that are helpful to consider. One is that certain emotions are based on comparison. Arrogance depends on comparing myself to others, believing I'm more intelligent, and because of that, more important. In admiration, I have the desire to emulate someone in their way of being or the skill they've developed.

Envy has this characteristic. The first thing that is helpful to remember when we feel envy is that it is only surfacing because we're comparing our life to another's. If we redirect our focus to ourselves and put our efforts into what we care about and what brings us satisfaction, envy will fade. It will have no fuel.

It is also the case that we are not seeing the whole picture. The success we see another person experiencing in their career or business is only the tip of the iceberg. We have no idea what they have invested or how hard they've worked or how much they have suffered. We have only our limited perspective. A bit of humility can lower the intensity of envy.

One way to benefit from envy is to think of its purpose. Envy points out things in other people's lives that we believe would enhance our lives. When we think of it that way, it becomes fuel for us to create a life we love and are satisfied with. In the end, it doesn't matter if I achieve what another has achieved; it matters that I am content with my life. Envy helps me see what that life would look like. Embrace it!

Envy

Story: "I would like to have what that person has."

Impulse: Look for a way to include the thing I desire in my life

Purpose: Show us what we would like to have as part of our life that we do not

---

Source: "The Field Guide to Emotions" by Dan Newby and Curtis Watkins

REGRET

Regret has a great memory. She remembers mistakes as old as the hills as though they just happened yesterday, allowing her to nag me all day long. She always starts with "If only ..." She is exhausting!

Hello Emotions!

The first time I planted pumpkins, I did not know which flower was female and which was male. Seeing flowers bloom was a joy. Opening the door early in the morning, I saw many golden baby flowers and eagerly waited to see the fruits. Unexpectedly, in the evening all of the flowers were shriveled, flattened, lying flat. I was deeply disappointed. After that, each morning I picked them all and put them into a pot for my breakfast. No more waiting!

One bright morning I discovered a strangely large flower. It was one and a half times the size of the rest. Looking closely, I noticed this type of flower had a baby pumpkin at the base. So, the female pumpkin flower was similar to that of the bitter melon; there was a tiny bulge where it had just budded. I was excitedly hopeful!

Two days passed, the flower shrank, and the baby fruit shriveled up. The next day another female flower was ready to bloom. But like her sister, she did not bear any fruit. I Googled and Googled looking for answers. I read that the male pollen must be put onto the female pistil for pollination. Oh! Every morning the male flowers had all gone into my pot! There had been no chance for bees and ants to transfer the male pollen to the female pistil!

A few days later, there appeared a third female flower. Needless to say, this lady had a brilliantly successful pregnancy thanks to my matchmaking skill! The chubby pumpkin baby with a slim dark green waist resting his head on the pebbles looked so cute. Yet, I had not been able to celebrate with Joy more than five minutes when Regret raised her eyebrows:

"If only you had Googled many days earlier, you would have gotten three pumpkins," she said with contempt.

Joy left. I was tired. This lecture happened again and again. Every time I sat contemplating the baby pumpkin, Regret repeated, "If only …"

The other day I had just finished watering the plants when I discovered that my little friend loofah was crooked on one side. Looking closely, I noticed the little loofah's "spine" was almost broken because of the strong stream of water coming from the garden hose sprayer. Regret crossed her arms, looked at me with a scowl, and said,

"You should have watered him gently with a small mug. He's still a tiny plant, but you sprayed him with the garden hose nozzle."

"He's been growing up," I said. "He's no longer tiny. It's just that his leaves are too fat and his spine broke when he tilted."

"Well, you should have anticipated this situation," Regret said, accusing me.

Aha! Today Regret told me I was responsible "to anticipate all possible situations."

She chastised me constantly, annoyingly insistent on staying at home. She sat beside the little loofah. Every time I passed by, she grunted loudly even though I had banked up more soil to help the loofah stand firmly. "He will die because of you!" she spat!

The baby loofah did not die. He became the second strongest among his siblings thanks to my special care adding soil, wood ash, and manure every week.

After giving birth to the little pumpkin, my pumpkin plant no longer produced female buds. She did not stretch out like her sisters either. All the nutrients she absorbed were used to take care of her only child.

Finally, Regret left in shame. She came to realize that she had tried to provoke regret about these things in vain.

I learned that there are things in life that would not change, even if I was able to travel back in time to try something different. There are unexpected events that happen to help us make better choices. What comes must surely come. What I did, what I had chosen, was the best I could, within my knowledge at that moment.

Now every time Regret comes to visit, I only need to smile softly and say: "Regret, I saw you," and she winks and leaves.

That was my experience with Regret. How about yours?

▶ *What do you regret in your life?*
▶ *What made you believe that you could have made a different choice given who you were at that time?*
▶ *Are you ready to forgive yourself and use Regret to shape your future?*

DAN'S THOUGHTS

Regret is a curious emotion because it is built on some suppositions that do not hold up to scrutiny. When I regret, it is because I believe that the present would be better if I had done something differently in the past. Sometimes I regret something I did and sometimes I regret *not* doing something, but the belief is the same.

One false belief underlying regret is that "I could have done something differently than I did," that I had a choice. That may be true, but generally we act as we do because, at the time, it makes the most sense to us. We do not act against our beliefs of what is best. So, although I hypothetically had the freedom to choose otherwise, I could not have, given who I was at that moment. Only later when I saw other possibilities did I believe I could have made a different choice.

The other falsehood embedded in regret is believing we know that life would be better if we had or had not done x. We do not know that. We believe it to be true, but have no idea whether a different path would have produced a better present.

Regret is a bit deceptive. It is not wrong to consider our previous ignorance or to have the desire that things had turned out better, but blaming ourselves for willfully making a poor choice is not necessary or productive. Our impulse is sometimes to berate ourselves for our stupidity or blindness, rather than appreciating that we now have new eyes and can see the world more clearly and fully.

Regret

Story: "If I had it to do over, I would do it differently."

Impulse: To wish I'd done something differently

Purpose: Let us reflect on the wisdom of past choices in order to make better ones in the future

---

Source: "The Field Guide to Emotions" by Dan Newby and Curtis Watkins

JOY

Joy possesses a megawatt smile and sparkling eyes. She rarely walks but instead dances, rarely talks but sings, infusing everyone around her with positivity and delight. A life with Joy is full of laughter. Her ecstatic energy is contagious. If you ask around, there's hardly anyone who doesn't like Joy. But when I told this to Joy, she simply shrugged.

"That's what people say, Thao, but I'm often stood up. Only Boredom stays with me in those moments."

"Huh?" I was stunned.

"Look nowhere else. You stood me up countless times."

"Really?"

"You were a workaholic when you were in the corporate world. You often promised me, 'Joy, wait for me to finish this important project. I promise to go out with you.' Every day you worked so hard on your project. The ongoing project hadn't yet been finished when the second and third one came. Your to-do list was unlimited. Once when you successfully delivered a huge project, I asked, 'Shall we throw a party?' You said, 'We're sure to celebrate over the weekend.' I waited. The weekend came and you were suffering from the stress of a new project. No time for fun.

"The times you were promoted—the first time, the second time, the third time. Have you ever gone to celebrate? Whenever I came, you said, 'Being promoted means earning even more trust from my new bosses. I have to work twice as hard.'

"Then you received a recognition letter from the biggest boss in the organization. I asked, 'Shall we celebrate?' but you answered, 'There are many other people who have gotten similar compliments from him. It's nothing to be happy about.'"

Joy left. I sat in awe. After many years working with complete passion, being trusted by my bosses, respected by my business partners, I rarely had pictures taken with Joy. My memory was full of stressful moments and challenging situations, unfinished goals and shortcomings that needed to be fixed. It explained why at the moment I stood at the crossroads on my career path, Confidence and Courage were not there for me but Anxiety, Fear, and Self-doubt were. There were a few times when I got lost and didn't know where to go.

Self-confidence is a firm, solid trust in your abilities. That Trust is built on evidence. Evidence must be made of beautiful, joyful moments of victory, of moments when we are proud of ourselves. As for me, I kept running, climbing, striving without ever stopping to recognize myself or reward myself with small things to energize the long journey.

That is my story with Joy years ago. What about yours?

▶ *What role is Joy playing in your work and life?*

▶ *When does Joy come to visit but you don't have time for her?*

▶ *When do you put her off "until there is something worth celebrating"?*

DAN'S THOUGHTS

Joy requires acknowledgment. This is the core truth in what Thao has shared. We live in a world where action is rewarded and considered more important than being. We rarely stop to focus on a sunset for the joy of the moment. We are more often working, preparing dinner, or watching a television program.

Joy is all around us. It is telling us that something good is happening or has happened. It is urging us to gather others and celebrate that moment of goodness. When we don't, the moment passes and joy goes with it. Joy is acknowledged through celebration.

There is a human tendency to ritualize joy to be sure we take time for it. We celebrate the goodness of birthdays, weddings, graduations, and certain holidays. We focus on the larger joys in life. What we often overlook are the small moments when we experience the goodness of life; the moment we first taste a favorite food, the smell of a lilac flower, the singing of birds.

Joy comes to visit often but may find your door closed and locked. What practice would allow you to stop and notice the small moments of joy that regularly occur? How can you make them visible? How can you acknowledge them and reap the joy that is growing right outside your door? It is up to you. Joy is already doing its part.

Joy

Story: "Life is amazing!"

Impulse: To celebrate

Purpose: Let us celebrate moments of goodness

Source: "The Field Guide to Emotions" by Dan Newby and Curtis Watkins

HATE

Hate is absurd. He cherishes values such as sincerity, honesty, integrity, and kindness. Whenever he notices someone ignoring those values, he immediately consigns them to a "not welcome" zone. It doesn't matter who the person is, how they behave in different contexts, or what makes them behave as they do. They are all banished even if they only violated his values once. Over time, the "not welcome" zone becomes more and more crowded since the offenders' friends are sent there as well.

Hello Emotions!

One day, at the end of the year, I met a former colleague. She had just moved to a new company and took a higher position leading a large department. She sought my support to help unlock her team's potential through their development. The company's budget was limited. We therefore agreed that I would help facilitate half a dozen pro bono workshops. Our plan was that after the pilot ended, her team would be invited to share in a video if they believed their learning had a significant business impact.

The agreement was sealed. The ex-colleague started to make arrangements. I accelerated my ongoing projects so I would be available. It was the end of the year, a time everyone who works in coaching and training knows is hectic. I worked nonstop until, suddenly, I fell ill for three weeks. I could do nothing but lie on my bed groaning with fever, drag myself out of bed to the kitchen to make soup, and get to the clinic to see a doctor for my sore throat and raging fever.

All of my workshops, training classes, and coaching sessions had to be postponed or canceled. Clients who understood my situation were willing to reschedule. Those who were not able to change the timing of their events ended their contracts. That was the first time I understood and experienced the importance of well-being for a solo start-up owner. When I worked for my former employer and didn't feel well, I took sick leave with the encouragement and care of my bosses and colleagues. The company covered all hospital and related medication fees, and I was entitled to full salary and bonus. On my coaching journey, whenever I was sick, I would have to take care of myself and everything else as well.

I couldn't blame anyone but me. I deserved it because of my workaholic habits. I had forgotten to listen to my body and take good care of myself. The painful experience of those three tiring weeks helped me make a firm commitment to a more relaxing work plan: Only commit to a fixed number of coaching sessions and seminars each week.

Once the plan was done, I panicked, remembering my promise to my former colleague. If I had delivered all the seminars for free for her team, my income would have dropped by more than half in two months. The best I could do was help facilitate a workshop for her direct reports. I sat at my desk, preparing an email for her. I struggled to find the words I wanted, and once they emerged on my screen, immediately they were deleted by someone. Turning my head, I saw Hate frowning and scowling:

"We ended our relationships with people who didn't fulfill their promises. Why are you doing this now?"

I was silent. For the first time, I realized that values are not just right and wrong. Those are the two extremes, "not at all" and "perfect." Committing to living the values you hold dear is a journey in pursuit of perfection. Not being able to live in accordance with our values in a certain situation does not mean that we are disregarding them.

And I accept that I'm only on the path to perfection. At this point, I have not reached the perfect milestone as I once believed I had. Accepting my imperfections also helps me accept other people's imperfections, and my "not welcome" zone is now nearly empty.

▶ *Has Hate ever visited you?*

▶ *What did he whisper to you?*

▶ *What will you do to make your "not welcome" zone less populated?*

DAN'S THOUGHTS

A common understanding of hate includes that we wish ill or want to hurt the other person. That perspective is why we've invented the term "hate crime." But hate has a different literal meaning, "to have a passionate aversion to."

Our impulse in hate is not necessarily to hurt the other person, but it is always to avoid them or to move as far away as possible. When we see someone we hate in the street, we turn away or hide our face so they will not see us. At all costs, we want to avoid an encounter.

Not all emotions have an opposite. Hate does. Its opposite is affection, which is the desire to be in another's presence simply because it is enjoyable. We want to get close and stay close, to be with them.

Understanding hate in this way can make it more "acceptable" or useful. When I hate someone, I am not judging them to be a bad person; I'm simply saying I want to avoid their presence. I find it disagreeable for some reason and do not see the value. In this interpretation hating someone does not make me a bad person any more than having affection for someone makes me a good person.

We learned the meaning of individual emotions from our parents, culture, and experiences. The interpretation we have is malleable. We can reexamine our understanding and adjust or shift it. Hate is one emotion for which that is a useful exercise. It may prompt you to consider making peace with the emotion of hate so it can help you understand yourself and others more fully.

Hate

Story: "I cannot stand being around this person or in this situation."

Impulse: To avoid similar situations or people

Purpose: Distinguish who we don't want to be near or what we don't want to be part of

---

Source: "The Field Guide to Emotions" by Dan Newby and Curtis Watkins

Hello Emotions!

LOVE

Do you remember the first time you opened your first reader? I remember that rainy evening, sitting on my bamboo bed, longing for my brother to return from the bookstore with mine. That moment is etched into my memory. Every minute waiting for him was like a decade. I sat restlessly, wondering if he was wandering around on his way home from the bookstore.

Finally, he arrived home. The moment I touched the book, excitement ran wildly down my neck and plunged into my tummy. "Oh, why did Mother say I would be able to read all the bedtime stories by myself if I had this book?" It seemed that the letters of the alphabet knew "my face," but I didn't know any of theirs. Disappointed, I couldn't do anything but wait for the first day of school.

The day I was able to remember each alphabet's "face" finally arrived. I took advantage of my new skill by reading them all, at any time, anywhere I found them. Grandma asked to read her news, I read! My uncle's huge piles of thick books, I read! Dad's Youth News, I read!

We could not afford children's books, but I was a bookworm, so I voraciously digested adult books and newspapers instead. Sunday

Hello Emotions!

Youth News, which had a short story page, was my favorite. I read, dreamt, and wrote my stories, then secretly placed my letter in the iron mailbox standing on the other side of the road where the postman came to collect mail every day. I waited and waited, but my stories were never printed in the newspaper. "I might have forgotten to put a stamp on my letter," the little kid in me might have wondered.

Writing brings pure joy to me. It doesn't take great effort for me to call forth words, probably thanks to my long-term "relationship" with them since childhood. Beautiful words, however, do not always come when I call them. There are days I can only sit in front of my laptop and wait. Meaningful words, the ones that can express my thoughts clearly, simply disappear. The more I try to write, the more I struggle. Every single word and sentence seems shallow, ugly, and meaningless.

Then there are days when sentences, words, and ideas pour nonstop from my fingertips without effort. I sit still, beaming brightly and watching in disbelief the dance of words, moving to and fro, arranging themselves in each sentence and paragraph. "Wow! I couldn't find you guys yesterday. What brought you all here now?" It feels like someone is writing for me. That someone has traveled back into my childhood, bringing me the pure joy I used to treasure.

One morning, after a challenging coaching session, I closed my laptop and walked out into the yard to get some fresh air. In a garden planter, my little coriander was about to fall over. They had grown so fast, it was hard for the porous soil to support them. I put on gloves, scooped up more soil, spread it evenly around them, and then pressed gently on the roots of the coriander. The feeling of my hands touching the ground, the tiny stems, the slender leaves, and the fragrance of the newly grown coriander warmed my heart. Hearing my heart sing and dance for a while, suddenly I grinned like an idiot.

How silly I was! How come the coriander became strangely lovely, the sun seemed brighter than usual, the bird's songs sounded more cheerful, the wind smelled cooler and more fragrant? Looking over, someone else was playing with the coriander:

"What's your name? You look both strange and familiar. I've been seeing you a lot lately. You usually come when I write blogs," I asked with a massive grin.

Hello Emotions!

"You don't know my name. You misname me all the time. Sometimes you call me Excitement, other times Passion, and then Happiness. My name is Love. I only appear when you truly appreciate, care for, and cherish someone or something simply because they are who they are, without expecting anything else."

Oh. I thought Love was with me when my heart skipped a beat at the sight of a special someone when I was 17, or when I was working day and night at the company office in my twenties and thirties. It turns out Love doesn't take that much effort. Love is simple and gentle.

Then it dawned on me that Love was the "culprit" urging me to pursue my coaching journey without considering the potential risks. That explained why I always get confused when someone admires the courage I had to change my career after ten successful years in market research. Courage means taking the plunge after considering all the risks. The truth is, I didn't foresee any risks. I simply followed the call of Love.

I fell in love blindly, but I have no regrets. Because the farther I go, the more I cherish[1] each experience, feeling grateful for being able to live fully in every moment on this journey.

- ▶ *Have you ever loved something without regrets?*
- ▶ *Are you listening to the message of Love?*
- ▶ *What is Love telling you?*

---

[1] Cherish: to love somebody/something very much and want to protect them or it. (Oxford Dictionary).

DAN'S THOUGHTS

No emotion has inspired as many stories, films, or conversations as love. But, even with all that attention, it is difficult for most people to say precisely what love is. How is it different from cherishing, liking, attraction, infatuation, passion, yearning, or longing for another person? And is it just about other people? What about self-love? What about the love of the land or a book or a sea breeze?

English is a rich language, but the possibilities it offers to articulate love are poor. Latin, Hindi, and other languages have much more precise ways of speaking about love. "Unconditional positive regard" is the way American psychologist Carl Rogers articulated it. It has been described as being always "patient, respectful, and kind," without "jealousy, resentment, or judgment." "Deep affection" is often considered a synonym.

A question many of us wonder about is "Where does love come from?" Some people chase love, others fall in love, and some are blindsided by love. Do we wait for it or go look for it? Will it find us?

I equate love with acceptance of a person as they are. When I love, I do not feel the desire to change or "improve" them. They are a legitimate human being and have the right to be as they are at this moment. I find that sometimes I do not like people I love, or at least I don't like certain things they do, yet remaining committed to them, honoring their legitimacy, and treating them with respect seem to be the hallmarks of love.

Love

Story: "I cherish you just as you are."

Impulse: To honor and cherish

Purpose: Accept the other as they are

Source: "The Field Guide to Emotions" by Dan Newby and Curtis Watkins

PASSION

Passion is an international celebrity!

While hundreds of his friends in the emotional world have been misnamed or classified into confusing groups such as Stress (representing all unpleasant emotions), Happiness (describing the community of pleasant emotions), and Emptiness or Normality (symbolizing the rest of other emotions), everyone in my country knows Passion, calling his name clearly in both Vietnamese and English.

Hello Emotions!

People not only know Passion, but they also love him. Befriending him is the most important item on everybody's wish list, from the fresh, innocent graduate to the senior, experienced CEO. The presence of Passion in anyone's interview is an essential prerequisite to being accepted and welcomed to the world of Facts and Figures.

Passion has a twin brother named Enthusiasm that only people with sharp eyes can distinguish. If Passion is full of energy, always longing to be involved in everything, Enthusiasm is persistent, resilient, and ready to live and die for his purpose in life.

Why Passion chose to befriend me as a small child remains a mystery. He motivated me to learn the alphabet, to master reading and writing, and to conquer numbers. He has shown me new ways of seeing and led me to areas that engage my mind for hours without getting bored. In his company, every day goes by in the blink of an eye.

The day I successfully deciphered the "secret letter of life," or my life's purpose, as many people call it, was the day Enthusiasm knocked on my door, insisting he needed to live there with his brother, Passion. Every day the two shouted and dragged me to my desk in the early hours of the morning. Daytime didn't seem to be enough; at night they visited my dreams, reminding me of their unending to-do list. One night I dreamt about coaching a client, asking her a powerful question, then awoke and jumped out of bed, searching for a notebook to write it down.

Passion

The consequence of working incessantly day and night, eating and drinking quickly, not exercising or resting led to a physical breakdown. There were occasions when I had to apologize to a client during a coaching conversation due to dizziness and lightheadedness. Exhausted, I threw Passion and Enthusiasm out of the house.

After the two of them left, the house became strangely quiet. Peace came to visit every day, urging me to meditate, relax, read books, go jogging, and rest. Peace invited Happiness and Joy. Together we enjoyed each moment and experienced the beauty of life.

I was getting healthier, but started feeling something was missing. I already had it all, the Peace and Happiness that the whole world was in search of, so why didn't I find it fulfilling? Why was I longing for something more? Was I too greedy?

One day I planned to visit Thai Plum Village. My friends warned me that I might not be able to adapt to the rhythm of the village, given that I was living at a hectic pace. At Plum Village, everyone learns to slow down to nurture Peace. I chuckled: "That will be a piece of cake. Isn't that what I am living now? This will be my vacation trip."

I arrived at Thai Plum Village when it was dark. Looking at the activities planned for the next day and those that came after, I was completely overwhelmed. Each day began at 4:00 a.m. so we would be ready for sitting meditation at 4:45, walking meditation at 5:15, followed by bamboo stick exercise, breakfast at

7, then listening to Dharma talk, lunch, naps, work together in the garden, group activities, exercise, dinner, dinner break, sitting meditation, and the day ended at 9 p.m., after an hour embracing thundering silence! No reminders would be given, but all activities were completed on time and in a harmonious manner.

"Military discipline" is one of the deep impressions left by my time at Plum Village. Looking at the leisurely steps, serene smiles, and compassionate eyes of the monks and nuns, I realized that they were the fruit of days of constant practice and discipline. That is what was required to be able to live mindfully in the present. And to be able to persevere, be resilient, and walk firmly on the path of enlightenment, the whole village knows that they are living the most meaningful purpose of life: helping people.

I found the answer to why I didn't feel fulfilled when I had Peace and Happiness.

I reopened my secret letter of life, called Enthusiasm to come back, and scheduled a team meeting to assign the scope of work for each member. Enthusiasm would go to work with me every day. Peace would come and gently close my laptop every 60 minutes, reminding me to take a break and use some of our precious time for gardening, meditation, reading books, or simply just resting. None would try to steal each other's time. Since that day Fulfillment has been visiting me more often at the end of each day.

I came to realize that Passion and Enthusiasm, Peace and Happiness are not opposite that exclude each other. We can live life fully with our ideals, our Passion, and still have Peace and Happiness by our side. For me to achieve Fulfillment, I must have both. How about you?

▶ *What is the role of Passion in your work and life?*

▶ *Have you ever let Passion overwhelm you?*

▶ *Which additional emotional friends will you invite to help you enjoy work and life to the fullest?*

DAN'S THOUGHTS

How we understand specific emotions has sometimes changed over the centuries. Originally, in Latin, passion meant *suffering*. In Christianity, it is linked to Jesus enduring crucifixion. In Middle English, it evolved to mean *a disease or affliction*. Finally, it became a way to describe a *deep desire or great admiration for another person*. In modern times we've often associated it with sexual attraction.

Passion is sometimes used to describe a wide range of other emotions, including zeal, grief, sorrow, rage, anger, hope, or joy. As we can see, it has always been seen as an intense emotion with deep roots.

If we wanted a single interpretation that could serve most purposes, I would propose that passion is "the desire to meld with another." If we lose ourselves in painting, we "become one" with it through the act. We may be passionate about music, sports, cooking, nature, or another person. Perhaps our passion is toward the divine or the universe. In all cases, we seek oneness with another.

For me, this is a lovely, respectful, profound understanding of passion that helps define my relationship with the world around me. What draws me in, invites me to immerse myself, and become one? What generates passion in your life? Where do you see it? How does it enrich who you are? What are you passionate about?

Passion

Story: "I have a deep desire to be a part of x."

Impulse: To be as close as possible

Purpose: Produce intimacy

Source: "The Field Guide to Emotions" by Dan Newby and Curtis Watkins

ENTHUSIASM

Enthusiasm's twin brother, Passion, is full of energy, always eager for a new journey, and keen to make things happen. He also quickly gets bored when the sense of newness has faded and easily gives up when facing obstacles. In contrast, Enthusiasm persists with mental toughness, persevering until the end of his journey. While the first rain shower discourages Passion, even thunderstorms only make Enthusiasm stronger.

Hello Emotions!

Passion loves making friends with anyone who is imbued with a burning curiosity and a strong desire for exploring their chosen field. However, befriending Enthusiasm requires one critical element: deciphering the Secret Letter of Life, written for each person when they are born, as it holds their Life Purpose.

Quite often I have met clients who sought my help to decode their Secret Letter of Life. Many showed up with Boredom, believing the answer would help them regain their energy at work. Some, accompanied by Envy, told me that all their colleagues and bosses had already found their purposes while they had not. A few brought Anxiety to our meeting, saying that if they could not understand the meaning of their letter, they would probably remain lost, pursuing a meaningless career for the rest of their life.

I knew why those clients entrusted me with this critical exploration. They had noticed that Enthusiasm and I had been joined at the hip since I started my coaching journey. The odd truth was that, at that time, how I had deciphered my Secret Letter of Life was a mystery. I didn't even know the answer revealed in that letter had a beautiful name: Life Purpose!

I read psychology books, listened to TED Talks, did information searches, and consulted different decoding approaches from numerous renowned authors and schools of thought. Looking back on it now, all those methodologies described exactly what I had been through and gave the same answer. One term that resonated deeply in my mind was "the crucible."

"The Crucible" is a condition, a situation, in which you have to endure painful experiences in the fierce heat of a fire, of severe hammering, and sufferings. All alone. You keep asking yourself why this has happened to you and no one else, what you did all wrong to be tested to such an extreme. Every passing day is filled with hopelessness, desolation, and despair. Then the moment you think there is no way out and you cannot stand it anymore, the solution appears.

"Life Purpose" is the answer to all the suffering you have gone through. The crucible is the place that makes you tough, strong, and mature. The moment you understand your Secret Letter, you desire to live up to your ideals of living a more meaningful life and making this world a better place to live.

It is difficult for you to abandon your ideals once you embark on your trip. There may be times when you are tempted to go back to living an easier life, there will be times when you are exhausted and times when you want to give up halfway through, but your heart won't let you. There are times when you complain, but most of the time you are grateful for choosing to pursue a journey that is meaningful to you.

Opening the Secret Letter of Life and finding my answer in the middle of the page, I couldn't help but wonder if I could have found the solution a few years earlier, and if I had, would I have dared to live up to my ideal? The answers are "No" and "No."

Without the "crucible," I would still be a workaholic, going to the office every day with Passion, still aimlessly socializing, and not caring much about the world. And if someone had helped me decipher my Secret Letter, it would have been too soon for me to have enough maturity, enough experience, and courage to live up to my Life Purpose.

Things happen for a reason. It is not necessary to rush decoding the Secret Letter. The solution will unfold at the right time and in the right conditions. That's what I have learned about my friendship with Enthusiasm and my Secret Letter of Life. What is your experience?

- ▶ *What "connection with the divine" or "higher purpose" have you not embraced?*
- ▶ *How could you?*
- ▶ *What would be the first step in making it your guiding star?*

DAN'S THOUGHTS

When our knowledge is limited, we group things into general categories. We see "a horse" rather than an Appaloosa, Belgian, or Arabian. A tree is just a tree; it isn't a pine, ginkgo, or maple. The same is true with emotions. When we have a small emotional vocabulary, we group several emotions under an umbrella. This happens with enthusiasm. We use it interchangeably, often with excitement, happiness, ambition, desire, and several other emotions.

Enthusiasm

If you had lived in Greece 2,500 years ago and you had a vision you believed was divinely inspired, you probably would have used the word *entheos* (in + god) to describe your emotion. Your vision was given to you or inspired by your connection with the divine. Today we use the word enthusiasm.

Understanding enthusiasm in this way elevates it above excitement or ambition. It acknowledges that sometimes we don't know where our vision of a future world comes from, and perhaps it is somewhere beyond us individually. Enthusiasm can help us see and speak about what we can see that others can't. It helps us share an idea that could remake society for the better.

How accessible is enthusiasm for you? Do you spend time reflecting and envisioning what could be? Do you invite support "from beyond" to connect and expand the possibilities you imagine? How would spending time in this unique emotion change the direction of your life?

Enthusiasm

Story: "I'm committed to a cause greater than myself."
Impulse: To act on behalf of a cause, mission, or vision greater than yourself
Purpose: Allow us to connect with and be energized by a purpose or mission greater than ourselves

---

Source: "The Field Guide to Emotions" by Dan Newby and Curtis Watkins

Hello Emotions!

BOREDOM

O f all the citizens inhabiting the world of emotions, Boredom is the guy I am scared of the most. I am not intimidated by him for who he is; I am frightened of his tricks. Whenever he shows up, he secretly locks all the doors, shuts all the windows, and hides. Sometimes he is alone with me, other times he asks a few of his more difficult friends to come play. Anxiety, Fear, and Resentment are Boredom's partners in crime. They all remain silent, which makes the house seem suddenly empty and suffocating.

Hello Emotions!

Lately, it was a huge surprise to me when I began experiencing emptiness quite often. I had successfully deciphered my Secret Letter of Life to discover my Life Purpose. Enthusiasm made a big commitment to travel with me anywhere I want, even venturing into unknown lands. Why was I suddenly experiencing emptiness? Why didn't I know what to do or where to go, and why had all my energy suddenly vanished into thin air?

After practicing emotional literacy for some time, I had learned some valuable lessons from my respected teachers, "There is no moment when we are not accompanied by an emotion. As human beings, we always have an emotion or mood. Emotions come and go when triggered, while moods are always with us and don't require a trigger." I sat meditating for a while, trying to calm my mind.

After a 30-minute meditation, I saw Boredom tiptoeing into the living room.

"Hey, Boredom, you are playing your tricks again. What brought you here today?" I asked, smiling.

"Ah! You're awake! I didn't hear any mental chatter, so thought you were asleep," he said. "Besides, I don't have anything else to do, and hide-and-seek is my favorite game when I feel this way." Boredom winked.

I was surprised. "I can't understand. We have many things on our plate right now, coaching contracts, workshops, and training classes. They are all exciting tasks we used to long for, and now you say that there is nothing here of interest? Is that what makes you bored? Tell me again what excites you."

"I don't know," he whined. "You need to tell me. I am just bored!"

"Give me the key so Enthusiasm can come back today and work," I shouted.

"No way, not until you tell me what will excite me," he shouted, and ran off to hide again where I couldn't find him.

Not being able to work, I picked up an inspirational book, hoping Boredom would go away when I finished. *The Promise of a Pencil* by Adam Braun sounded interesting. I read and read, and then something suddenly struck me. The author had a strong faith in his life-or-death situation. He wrote he had 100 percent conviction that it wasn't his time when his ship experienced a terrible storm on his first journey. Faith provided him with a wave of calm during that tough time.

"I want Faith!" I shouted in inspiration.

"Really? I thought you never wanted anyone to know we were friends." Somehow Faith had managed to open my window, shouting back.

I was stunned. Faith was so right. I couldn't lie to her. I had always felt embarrassed if someone knew she was my friend. Befriending Faith meant I was empowered to believe in something or someone without any evidence, and that sounded stupid. How could a person who was (and still is) famous for always backing up her statements with facts, figures, and logic have a friend like Faith?

But the moment I smiled at Faith and invited her into my house, I felt a surge of confidence, and all my energy rushed back. It dawned on me that day that without Faith, I didn't have enough confidence to achieve my dreams. I had countless exciting ideas and action plans to have a big impact on society that I dared not execute. I always played it safe and stayed in my comfort zone, convincing myself that was enough, and that is the reason Boredom visited frequently, reminding me that it was time to step into uncharted areas again. But this time I was not going alone. I had Faith!

Boredom threw the key on my lap. He laughed and disappeared, but I was sure he knew I was grateful for his valuable lesson.

That was my story with Boredom. My answer to his question was Faith. Many clients of mine tell me their answer is Courage, Gratitude, and sometimes Acceptance. What's yours?

- ▶ *What did you experience when Boredom visited?*
- ▶ *What did it lead you away from and what possibility did it open?*
- ▶ *How could you listen to and embrace Boredom to live a richer life?*

DAN'S THOUGHTS

By habit, we categorize emotions as positive or negative, and boredom generally gets assigned as the latter. I imagine that is because we don't see the value of boredom that Thao articulated in her story. Its linguistic root comes from the idea of "boring a hole," and we believe that holes are nothing but empty spaces.

But holes are essential. They allow us to plant trees, employ buttons, and have swimming pools. So, perhaps our disregard for them should be reconsidered. A more useful way of thinking about boredom is simply that I'm not seeing what in this situation could be of value to me. Perhaps there isn't anything, but maybe I'm just not seeing it.

Boredom has the essential role of directing our attention and energy to things that we find interesting and believe could be helpful for us to experience or learn. Its partner in this effort is curiosity, which we could consider its opposite. Curiosity is provoked when we see something we believe is of value to us and generates the desire to know more. Boredom redirects us, and curiosity engages us.

The next time you're bored, pay attention to what it is telling you. Consider whether the thing you're bored with has no value or you're blind to its potential value. Get curious about your boredom, and you will find that it is much more interesting than you ever imagined.

Boredom

Story: "There is nothing here of interest to me."

Impulse: To look for something else to do, disengage

Purpose: Move us away from things of little perceived value

Faith

Story: "I believe it even though I don't have evidence it is true."

Impulse: To commit to a belief

Purpose: Allow us to believe without the need for evidence

Source: "The Field Guide to Emotions" by Dan Newby and Curtis Watkins

STRESS

A very bad boy named Corona was on his summer vacation with plenty of time on his hands, so he wanted to play hide-and-seek.[2] I did not have time for his games, but felt I had no choice but to yield to his demand.

"It's okay, I have played this game many times before," I thought to myself.

Day by day I hid well. I no longer wandered the streets or around the shopping malls. I occupied myself within my little house. I kept myself busy with workshops, coaching contracts, and a dozen other exciting projects, such as blogging and podcasting. My schedule was full from dawn to dark. It was a good way to forget about my annoying little "friend," who shouted nonstop, "Five… ten… fifteen… twenty…" out there.

I tried to maintain my usual healthy diet, smiled brightly every time I met clients, and maintained my calm and lighthearted chitchat with friends. "I'm fine" or "I'm great" was my default response whenever someone asked, "How are you? Are you okay?"

---

[2] Covid-19 is personified here as a bad little kid.

Hello Emotions!

"I am fine" seemed to be the message from my will, because my body did not agree. The earliest sign was a tightness in my abdomen, which I suffered while meditating. My belly felt like an inflated balloon, causing each breath to be painful. Then my stomach went on strike, refusing to digest food. There were nights I could only sleep three or four hours because of the discomfort. My energy gradually drained away. I couldn't work anymore, and that was when I truly felt the ebb.

Lying on my bed with a weary body and painful stomach, my mind could not run away from work anymore. As a result, all the worries and fears that I'd been ignoring and neglecting for so long came rushing in.

Anxiety began, "All your friends have done their packing, ready to quarantine if necessary, but you haven't made your list, you haven't bought anything. How can you respond in case of an emergency?"

Fear shouted, "The neighborhood coordinator has just asked you to get a test. I heard it's crowded at the testing location. You better be careful. By the way, your district has just been locked down and your refrigerator is empty. If there are no vegetables for your mother, her blood sugar will spike."

Anxiety interrupted, "A client has requested a full-day workshop with a sixty-minute lunch break. I am sure that won't be enough time for you to recuperate. What do you think?"

Listening to what Anxiety and Fear said, I felt like a donkey. Every morning I woke up feeling a huge responsibility. The workload did not decrease and even increased gradually over the years. And now I had to strain to carry an even heavier load due to the fears and concerns that little Corona sneakily weighed me down with. Never had I felt so much weight on my shoulders; never had I felt so tired, lonely, and helpless.

I quietly let go of the story that "I'm always strong." I had tried to carry on with that belief every day. I accepted that I was stressed. I admitted that I needed help.

With a little hesitation, I texted my Mindfulness Lovers group and asked, "Are you okay, guys?" To my surprise, the messages that appeared said things like, "I'm not feeling well" or "What a coincidence, I'm not so good. I'm glad you asked." From there we shared our difficulties. I felt a release, knowing that I was not alone with all the difficulties that I was facing.

Then I decided to "complain" a bit with my close friends of more than ten years, telling them that I had just borrowed vegetables from a neighbor because my family had run out of food. Surprisingly, they didn't mind listening to my moaning; they even asked if they could have their food delivered to my place.

The Global Brand Director, after learning that I needed a three-hour lunch break, quickly agreed. He said, "It makes sense. You have to be attentive to each person in the workshop. That must be exhausting."

Little Corona hadn't gotten tired yet. He was still excited about playing his game. Many challenges were still ahead, but I felt the warmth of care and love of my friends and even from strangers.

I gradually regained my energy and the desire to work, but this time I approached it more wisely. I promised myself that I would listen to every little change in my body, love myself more, and take time to rest and meditate when I felt the very first sign of stress.

The big lesson I have learned is that I do not have to become the sun or the moon to warm and illuminate the whole planet. I just need to be a small fire. When I'm strong enough, my fire will warm up the cold places. And when it goes out, I will have the courage to ask for some fire from people around me.

▶ *Have you ever experienced Stress? What have you learned?*

▶ *What emotions would allow you to lower the level of Stress you feel?*

▶ *What is your daily routine and practice to invite these emotions into your life?*

DAN'S THOUGHTS

Stress is often thought of by people as an emotion, but if you stop to examine it, you'll find that many emotions trigger stress. I find it more useful to think of stress as something that happens to your body when those emotions are present. We easily link stress to anxiety or fear, but it also appears in uncertainty. And it shows up when we are excited or in awe.

Stress from this perspective generally refers to the contraction of our muscles. It may cause us to stop breathing (for a moment) or to take shallow breaths. We may hesitate or the contraction of muscles can allow us to run when necessary.

There is a related emotion that can be helpful to distinguish, which is strain. It occurs when stress surpasses the capacity of the system (in this case, you) to tolerate it. The result in physical terms is that something breaks. So, while stress is essential to living, strain damages us in some way. This is the difference between exercising a muscle or tearing one.

When a part of us has been strained, it takes time to recover and may require medical attention.

Stress can be relieved in a number of ways. Using breath as a tool is among the most useful. Intentionally breathing more deeply relaxes the body and allows anxiety to quiet itself. Another method is to exaggerate the tension in your shoulders, for instance, then immediately relax them. That "letting go" of tension reduces your stress. Another possible stress-reliever is changing your environment. Going for a stroll through a quiet forest lessens stress for most of us, although if it generates an emotion like fear, you'll find it increases stress.

We all can find techniques or practices that allow us to be more intentional about the stress we are carrying. We know that unhelpful stress will show up, so experimenting with methods that allow you to navigate it is an excellent investment of time. It gives you choice.

HOPE

One night while I was counting sheep, Misery and Terror slouched into my room hugging their pillows. They both looked pale and haggard. I thought, "They must be preoccupied with something and finding it difficult to fall asleep."

"What happened? You two told each other late-night stories and now can't sleep, right?" I moved back a bit to let them climb onto my bed.

Misery: "It's not me this time. It's Terror. Today he spent all day tracking the number of infections in our hometown and then going to Facebook groups to read some doctors' advice on how to treat coronavirus patients at home. He immersed himself in bad news and brought it up at bedtime. How could anyone sleep after listening to all those sad and scary stories?"

Terror defended himself: "This fourth outbreak is terrifying. Right now our city has reached the stage where many infected people must be treated at home. I'm certain something horrible is going to happen."

Hello Emotions!

I gave Terror a stern look. "Terror, you are naughty! You are not allowed to touch your phone anymore.

"Come here, I'll read you guys a story to put you to sleep."

Putting the sheep I'd be counting aside for later, I reached for my Kindle to read *The Islanders* by Mary Alice Monroe. It tells the story of a beautiful and peaceful summer vacation of three kids, Jake, Lovie, and Macon, on Dewees Island.

I read, *"At the point where the turtle nest was moved because of the coyote's attack, the children worried whether the coyote would find the new location. Jake's grandmother said, 'We just have to hope, child. What's life without hope?'"*

As I read that passage, something got stuck in my brain. For some reason, my hand would not turn to another page and I kept muttering: "Hmm ... what's life without hope?"

"Did you call me?" Hope poked his head into the room where the three of us were lying.

"No ... oh yes. Hope, I am wondering, what would life be like without you in this world?"

Hope pushed open the door, grinning: "Who told you that there would come a time when I would no longer be in this life? That will never ever happen. My presence is the law of life!"

"What does that mean?" I trembled with excitement.

"Have you not realized that night is always followed by dawn and that no matter how scary the storm is, the sky will always clear? What you have been experiencing in your life is the same.

When you lost your first job, you thought the whole world was falling apart. You cried day and night, but then you got an offer that gave you a great chance to work and live with all your passion. Many years later you had to leave everything behind, and again you believed it might be the end of the world, and you are now living your ideal life to the fullest every day.

"Life is like a mountain-trekking journey. When you reach the lowest point, just push a little harder and you will rise. Just a little bit more. There is no other way to go but up, even if you want to go lower.

"My name is Hope, but I'm not just Hope. I am not the illusion of the light at the end of the tunnel in the darkest hours. I am not the optimistic thoughts that make people live in the clouds to forget the hard reality. I am the law of this life!"

My whole body started to relax. My eyelids fell. Before falling asleep, I saw Hope gently opening my bedroom door to let Misery and Terror out.

- *Have you experienced moments of Hopelessness or Despair?*
- *In your darkest moments, do you believe in Hope?*
- *What will you do next time to invite Hope into your challenging moments?*

DAN'S THOUGHTS

Hope is an emotion that is often misunderstood or even dismissed as wishful thinking. But hope has an essential role in life. Hope is the emotion that allows us to conceive of and work toward a future that we believe will be better than the present or past. It is the emotion that gives us the energy to seek out new possibilities.

When we lose hope and fall into hopelessness or despair, it is debilitating because we have nothing to aspire to or pursue. We are stuck in the present without any emergent possibilities. In those moments the questions that often show up are, "Why bother? Why try? What difference will it make? I cannot improve my life."

Humans need a vision "to live into." Hope allows us to imagine a future that gets us excited, engaged, and enthused. What hope can do for us is point to the path. From there, we need to bring ambition, boldness, or adventurousness to the fore to move ahead, but none of those would have value without hope setting the direction.

Hope

Story: "I believe the future will be better than the present or the past."

Impulse: To look to the future

Purpose: Allow us to envision a better future

Source: "The Field Guide to Emotions" by Dan Newby and Curtis Watkins

Hello Emotions!

IMPATIENCE

mpatience and Excitement, though they are not from the same family, are more than blood brothers. They are inseparable whenever they come to my house, and I only notice too late that their presence comes with a price tag.

The moment we agreed to co-write *Hello Emotions!*, Excitement shouted loud and clear, "This is your first book ever!

Your childhood dream is going to come true soon! And what's more, you will be co-writing it with one of your most respected teachers! I can't wait to get started. Yippee!" We both jumped and danced and grinned from ear to ear and immediately made a detailed plan.

Excitement had joined me at the hip since that day. He made the book-writing project my top priority regardless of how busy my calendar was. He made me obsessed with it. The book was the first thing in my thoughts the moment I woke up. It was the only thing on my mind during my morning meditation session, it followed me on my running route, it was present during each mealtime, and it made it hard to sleep every night.

Normal working hours weren't enough, Excitement urged me to cut short my rest time for the project. With Excitement's presence, it felt like my energy had been boosted and that I could conquer anything I wanted, that I could work day and night without feeling tired. My mind was driven by Excitement, but my body didn't agree. It went on strike, starting with a head-ache, then a stomachache, and then my whole body collapsed. It simply wanted to lie in bed doing nothing.

It took me almost two weeks to recover. The moment I could touch my laptop again, Excitement came back. "Hey, let's continue. We are almost a month behind schedule."

I looked askance at Excitement. "How could that be? We only stopped working on it about two weeks ago."

"But it feels like a month to me, Thao. I am always here, ready for you, and I am tired of waiting!"

"Wait a minute! This doesn't sound like you, Excitement. You don't normally rush me. What is happening?"

"Hmm … You are right. It is Impatience. He told me to push you, just a bit," Excitement murmured apologetically. Then he shouted, "Impatience, no hiding anymore. She knows you're here. We need to talk."

Impatience slowly emerged from my pantry, smiling sheepishly. "It is just a thought, Thao."

I smiled at him, "Impatience, imagine if we finished everything today. What would we do then?"

Impatience was speechless for a moment. "Oh, I hadn't thought of that. But from what I have observed of you in the past few decades, you feel bored as soon as you deliver a project. Then you have to brainstorm a new project to get Excitement to come back and work with you. Then you rush to finish that new project. Am I right, Excitement?"

Excitement nodded. I was silent. Excitement and Impatience quietly walked out my door, leaving me alone with all my thoughts.

Impatience's incisive observation left me speechless. I used to yearn for the energy of Excitement, trying so hard to brainstorm new ideas to have his companionship. I used to blame my body for its weakness, not giving me enough energy to work on the projects I loved. I used to blame Boredom for showing up too quickly. But today I saw the root problem—that I always rushed to the finish line and wasn't able to enjoy each moment on my journey. My body became heavy with relaxation. I knew what I should do.

I emailed Dan, asking him the deadline he had in mind for the book. To my surprise and relief, he replied that he did not have a deadline. He said that co-writing this book was a gift to him and he was truly enjoying each day he worked on it.

That was one of my experiences with Excitement and his closest friend, Impatience.

- ▶ *Do these two ever visit you together?*
- ▶ *What lessons have you learned from them?*
- ▶ *Are you able to choose which will serve you best when you notice them both?*

DAN'S THOUGHTS

When we feel impatience, it isn't unusual for us to interpret it as meaning that something is wrong or somebody is to blame. But are those true? Think about a moment when you felt impatient. Perhaps you were waiting to leave the house and the person going with you wasn't quite ready. Maybe you were waiting for the bus that seemed to never come or were stuck driving in heavy traffic.

If you reflect on these and similar situations, you'll notice something they all have in common. You are ready for something to happen, but other people or the conditions you are in are not. In this interpretation, impatience has more to do with alignment of readiness than right and wrong.

When we hold to the moral interpretation of impatience—I'm right and the other person is wrong—we create a barrier that is difficult to surmount. We feel in the right because "we were ready on time" or "we have a schedule to meet" and we look for someone to be wrong.

With all emotions, impatience included, we can determine the interpretation we are going to live by. It is up to us to determine which interpretation will be most useful for us and most supportive of the relationships we care most about.

Impatience

Story: "I am ready, but others are not."

Impulse: To look for a way around whatever is blocking you

Purpose: Get into action

Source: "The Field Guide to Emotions" by Dan Newby and Curtis Watkins

Hello Emotions!

SYMPATHY

Compassion, Empathy, and Sympathy belong to the same family. The eldest, Compassion, is famous for having a big heart, always rushing to help if she knows someone is in need. She puts others' minds at ease just by her presence. Empathy has a knack for sensing what others are feeling, which helps them love being around

her. Sympathy is not as gifted as her sisters. She needs real experience to understand how others feel. She struggles to follow her sisters and give a helping hand, and sometimes makes the situation worse.

On my last trip to Dalat, before the Covid outbreak, the bus I was on stopped at a small restaurant so everyone could take a short break. I wandered around to stretch my legs and noticed a blind man selling lottery tickets. He sat cross-legged in the corner. Sitting next to the seller was another young man, a customer. This person was going through the entire bundle of lottery tickets, reviewing each one carefully.

While we were queuing up, Hate whispered in my ear, "This customer should not choose only the tickets with the lucky numbers. That leaves only the bad ones. The seller is blind. How can the rest be sold? What is he thinking? I'm uncomfortable with this man."

I looked at Sympathy. "What do you think?"

"When it is our turn, we should support this seller as we often do with the elderly," Sympathy advised.

When the picky man left, I quickly chose two random tickets and gave the seller double the money, saying, "Brother, you don't need to give me the change. I'll take these two tickets."

The man looked hurt. He frowned at me. "No. You take your change and select your tickets carefully!"

The penny dropped. This seller was different from all the other unfortunate sellers I had met before. They were happy to receive more than they asked from their buyers. But this seller chose to work like regular people do and requested that others treat him as normal. The young man might be a frequent customer and had learned this, but I had judged him to be thoughtless.

Hate left. Sympathy and I carefully chose our tickets, took back the change, and thanked the seller. It was an eye-opening lesson for both of us, and we felt grateful for this learning experience. It has helped us open our hearts a little more and enrich our lives.

▶ *Have you ever been in a similar situation?*
▶ *What was your lesson?*
▶ *How could you strengthen Sympathy without it becoming Pity?*

DAN'S THOUGHTS

These three emotions—Compassion, Empathy, and Sympathy—give us unique ways to relate to other living things. One, empathy, gives us the ability to feel what someone else is feeling. It gives us a primal emotional connection with another person largely devoid of reason. We often say "we get" the other person or "feel their pain."

Sympathy lets us understand how another person is feeling because we've felt something similar. If I've been severely ill at some point in my life, I have some insight into how a gravely ill friend feels today. Sympathy provokes us to send flowers or cards to let the person know there is someone who understands their struggle.

Compassion allows us to legitimize the emotional experience another person is having. When we speak out of compassion, we acknowledge what the person is feeling and that it makes sense based on their interpretation of their experience. We are not necessarily agreeing with their interpretation or emotion, nor are we experiencing it at that moment. We are able to maintain our emotional center, which is often needed if we want to help them understand their situation differently. This is why compassion is such a valuable emotion for coaches, teachers, health-care workers, and people who support other people.

When we feel an emotion in this area, it is helpful to consider which will be most useful to the other person and to us. Compassion is not a replacement for empathy, and vice versa. If we want to care for our closest relationships in the most effective manner possible, we need clear distinctions between these three powerful emotions.

Sympathy

Story: "I have experienced something similar."

Impulse: To acknowledge others' emotions

Purpose: Let us identify with the emotions of another

Empathy

Story: "I am feeling what you are feeling."

Impulse: To share emotions with another

Purpose: Allow us to feel what others are feeling

Compassion

Story: "I am with you in your challenges."

Impulse: To be with another in his/her difficulty or pain

Purpose: Be with others in their pain or struggle

Source: "The Field Guide to Emotions" by Dan Newby and Curtis Watkins

Hello Emotions!

GENEROSITY

Generosity is born to give. He loves to share, take care, and he dedicates himself to helping others. His devotion to people in need is always a source of inspiration for people around him.

Everyone wants to be part of his work. Joy sends Generosity her sunny smile, being wrapped skillfully in each gift. Compassion and Love volunteer for the delivery job with care and courtesy. Anger makes receivers feel justice. Everybody in

the world of emotions finds a role in Generosity's campaigns, and Disappointment is no exception.

Disappointment is a secret admirer of Generosity. If she had one wish, it would be to be around Generosity as much as she can. She has been thinking hard about her present. It has to be unique, something special to remind Generosity of her wherever he goes. In the end, she has chosen what she most cherishes and wrapped it carefully in a beautiful gift box.

At first, Generosity and I didn't understand the implication of Disappointment's present. We innocently carried it around while helping others, and something strange began to happen.

After running a few fundraising campaigns, we noticed we were being followed by Resentment. He kept complaining that God was not fair, that we had sacrificed ourselves to live humble and selfless lives, and still we could not achieve what we wanted. On another day, after offering a free coaching program, I was confronted by Anger. He was so upset because the coachees did not bother to write a proper thank-you email and that they seemed to take my time and effort for granted.

Generosity and I were tired, wondering whether we were doing it all wrong. We sat in silence and stared blankly at our big present bag, which was now empty. A few moments passed before a small blue gift at the bottom caught our eye.

"Hey, what is this, Generosity? Did we forget to share a gift?" I asked in surprise.

Generosity picked up the cute little present, took a closer look, and said: "No, I don't think it is a gift for others. It says, 'To Generosity, this is my gift for you: Expectations. From Disappointment with love!'"

The penny dropped. We were speechless. Because of Disappointment's gift, what we had offered to others never completely selfless. Everything came with an expectation. When we did good deeds, we wished good karma would come as a reward. When we offered help, we expected others to feel grateful, at least. The presence of Resentment, Anger, and other uncomfortable emotional friends was the result of these hidden desires.

"Got it!" both of us shouted. "From now on, we will never include any expectations in our offers!" It worked better for a while, but one day something else happened.

That day, after teaching a free EQ class to help people overcome Fear during the time of Covid, I closed Zoom and felt drained. It was not because of the workload; it was the sight of Dissatisfaction.

"What's up, my friend?" I sighed. "This time Generosity and I checked carefully to be sure we didn't expect anything from others. Why are you here?"

"I know you guys did not expect anything from the people in your course, but you weren't going to be satisfied until all the participants found the solution they were looking for. And now, after one day of training, you see that only a few did," Dissatisfaction replied.

"What is wrong if we only want satisfaction?" Generosity sounded incredulous.

"It is still an expectation!" Dissatisfaction shrugged.

"Oh no! We tried our best! How could we refuse Disappointment's gift forever?" Generosity said quietly with despair.

"What if you need to accept that everyone wants to be part of your work? What if you need to accept that Disappointment is forever your fan and she will never give up sending her gift?" Someone popped his head through the window, joining our conversation.

"Oh, Acceptance! Welcome home!" I gushed. "You are right! If we cannot get rid of something, we have to accept its presence and find our way from there. From now on, we will keep our expectations in check and set them aside before helping others. If we are still visited by uncomfortable emotional friends, we will revisit our expectations and let them go as well."

Thanks to the special relationship between Generosity and Disappointment, I have learned a meaningful lesson: The path of selfless living is a journey. The more expectations I can let go of, the more I can enjoy my journey with Generosity.

- ▶ *Have you ever experienced a similar story between Generosity and Disappointment on your selfless journey?*
- ▶ *What has it taught you?*
- ▶ *What would you do to enjoy the path with Generosity to the fullest?*

DAN'S THOUGHTS

Generosity is, without a doubt, seen as a positive emotion. We even make it a feature of a person's character and morals. It is certainly invaluable in that it allows us to give freely from our resources, time, and energy. However, there are two important considerations before we crown Generosity as a "royal" emotion.

The first is the characteristic Thao illustrated in her story. True generosity comes without expectations. We give because we want to give, period. If there is a benefit for us, it is probably the satisfaction we feel when we have given without strings. It is the joy we see in the other person who has received something they needed and could not afford. This can take practice because we may have expectations that are subtle or well hidden.

The second thing to be aware of is that we can be generous in excess. Giving is good, but we can also impoverish or exhaust ourselves because we give so much. This can occur when the impulse to give is stronger than the impulse for self-care. Generosity can result in us automatically offering our time or resources without first checking whether the offer is in balance with the rest of our life.

Be generous, give freely, but don't forget your needs.

Generosity

Story: "I want to share what I have."

Impulse: To give

Purpose: Allow us to share our wealth or resources

Source: "The Field Guide to Emotions" by Dan Newby and Curtis Watkins

COMPASSION

Have you ever rushed to find a meeting room in the tense minutes just before a meeting? I have and it usually worked out, but I remember once when it didn't. Our office had many meeting rooms which led me to be overconfident one would be available when I needed it.

Hello Emotions!

That day, out of habit, I rushed to one of my favorites due to the nice view and natural light. It was available to all employees but was occasionally reserved for a visiting executive. A few days earlier I had seen a small note on the door saying the room was reserved for RJ. My colleagues told me this executive was in transit and would be in our office for a few weeks waiting for his official start date as chairman in an important North Asian country.

I looked at my phone. There were three minutes left before the meeting started and the room was empty. There was no laptop, no briefcase, only a half-drunk cup of water someone had left on the table. I was overjoyed thinking, "The boss probably won't come into the office today. This room is mine. Yeah!"

The moment I had dialed in, turned on the speakerphone, and started the conversation, RJ opened the door. Needless to say, I paled in Anxiety, Fear, and Embarrassment and my heart beat wildly. Immediately I got up, apologized, and was about to pack up my laptop. Very quickly, the executive, in a calm and stern voice, said: "I have booked this room, but you have started the meeting, so you stay, and I'll leave".

I was shocked by the RJ's decision. It was understanding, professional, quick, and decisive. He understood that I was in a stressful situation in which the meeting had already started and there was no other meeting room available. He did not think about his superior status, which gave him the right to use the room that had been reserved for him. Less than a minute after I encountered him for the first time, I could clearly feel his understanding, support, and respect.

This is the memory I shared at my farewell party when I was asked "Which bosses have left a lasting impression on you during your time working here?". To my surprise, everyone fell silent and was deeply touched by this simple story.

Compassion is an emotion that I once thought was only present in monks and nuns or people who did good deeds. I thought that there must be something wrong if Compassion showed in the workplace where soft and gentle emotions are not be allowed. Surely, Compassion would not meet the criteria to get into a multinational company where everyone lives in a fighting, winning spirit.

I've learned that in Compassion we don't need to do anything overtly emotional. A compassionate boss conveys the message, "I understand what you have been through, and I am with you in your challenges".

In my coaching journey, I have had the privilege of facilitating numerous workshops and listening to countless touching stories about my clients' line managers. From those, I've realized that Compassion is a magical emotion and has the power to create deep connections between a leader and their employees.

- ▶ When have you experienced Compassion in your workplace?
- ▶ What do you think about bosses who have shown Compassion for you?

Hello Emotions!

▶ Do you want to show Compassion to your team? What will you from today do to make Compassion part of your leadership?

DAN'S THOUGHTS

Compassion differs from empathy, sympathy, or pity. Our word compassion originated to describe being present with another person and witnessing their challenge. If you think about times people have stood by your side in compassion you will remember its power. Perhaps the other person said nothing, but somehow you knew they would not abandon you. They didn't advise or offer suggestions; they were simply present and legitimized what you were experiencing.

Compassion is the emotion we're often talking about when we say someone understands us. They may not agree with us, but they can see the situation from our perspective, which helps us confirm the validity of our experience. It also doesn't mean we are correct in our view.

We can practice compassion by clarifying and maintaining our emotional center, then listening deeply to how the other person's experience appears to them. We act as a witness to their experience and the way they see it but are not their cheerleader.

Compassion

Compassion is as important an emotion for leaders, educators, coaches, or care workers as empathy. In compassion, we are not necessarily trying to help overtly but are supporting the other person through our presence. Sometimes being is as valuable as doing.

Compassion

Story: "I'm with you in your challenges."

Impulse: To be with another in his/ her difficulty or pain

Purpose: Be with others in their pain or struggle

Source: *The Field Guide to Emotions* by Dan Newby and Curtis Watkins.

Hello Emotions!

Part 3

A FEW MORE FUN OBSERVATIONS
ABOUT OUR SPECIAL FRIENDS

Hello Emotions!

EMOTIONS NEVER COME ALONE

After observing emotions for a while, I realized that it is rare for a single emotion to visit me alone. When they come, many rush in. Some shout "hello" to distract me so their friends can sneak in the window or tiptoe through my back door. They love to hide so they can later come running out to wreak havoc on my peace, making me tired.

The ones I can see and hear clearly only reveal the tip of the iceberg, a part of the truth. Those hiding always withhold the biggest insights, and things can only be resolved by listening to what they have to say.

In the past, I was easily vulnerable to trifles. When I took coach training, there were numerous group assignments, so we formed a team of six on WhatsApp.[3] Members often texted to ask questions, and others in the group were always generous in giving help. Every time a group member forgot to say "thank you" for my help, I felt a nagging resentment and sometimes hatred.

---

[3] WhatsApp is a messaging app that allows you to send and receive messages and calls for free.

Hello Emotions!

By taking the time to quiet my mind and observe these emotional friends, I realized that Self-doubt was the emotion hiding behind Resentment and Hate. Every time the situation repeated itself, Self-doubt whispered into the ears of Resentment and Hate: "Your opinion has no value and your friends don't care whether you share."

After inviting Self-doubt to have a chat and listening to her carefully, I learned she was holding the long-standing belief that "all of my successes have come because of good luck." This belief had helped me continuously strive, but never allowed me to acknowledge my efforts. Self-doubt, therefore, had a reason to creep into my house very often without me noticing. I only saw Resentment and sometimes Hate on the surface of my suffering.

From the moment I discovered Self-doubt and gained this valuable insight into myself, I also had the solution: appreciate my efforts and acknowledge all my achievements, including the smallest. Since then, not only has Self-doubt stopped visiting me, but Resentment and Hate have never visited in similar situations.

▶ *Can you observe the emotional guests that come to visit you every day?*

▶ *Every time they come, can you decipher the interesting stories about yourself?*

▶ *And do you connect with their purpose or why they are visiting you?*

DAN'S THOUGHTS

A curious thing about two or more emotions showing up at the same time is that they sometimes seem contradictory, but on closer inspection, we find that they are not. For instance, when a close friend achieves something significant, we might feel both admiration and envy. In this case, admiration is saying, "If I ever do what he does, I'd like to do it the way he does." Envy is saying, "I wish I had achieved what he has."

They also have different purposes. Admiration, which means to "look up to," shows us role models that can inspire us. Envy tells us what we believe a good life would include, and this can generate ambition and energize our efforts.

In this situation, admiration and envy don't cancel each other out or even work against each other, although we may find their juxtaposition confusing. They each have their message to us and are trying to support us in their way. Our job is to listen to both, then decide what we will do with each.

Hello Emotions!

UNINVITED EMOTIONAL FRIENDS

There are hundreds of inhabitants in the world of emotions. Yet not all of them like to hang out with me, and those who do come do not stay the same length of time.

There are folks I rarely see, like Rebelliousness. There are those whom I have to diligently practice over time to strengthen my friendship with, such as Peace, Calmness, Courage, and Equanimity. And there are friends who come without invitation when they feel like visiting, and it's not easy to ask them to go. I have a few "best" friends like that, Anxiety and Self-doubt.

But it's not just me. Look around and see for yourself. Some people seem to easily lift the mood of people around them, some are overly serious, some are always compassionate toward others, some see the world through the lens of hate, some are reckless, some rarely take risks, some are overconfident, and some always doubt themselves.

The day I learned how to talk to emotions, I was able to make an action plan to stop worry and self-doubt. I began to live my days without worry and felt like I could conquer the whole world. I thought I would always be able to maintain that mood, but that is not the case. When I am busy with work, or even a little distracted, those two immediately slip into my house, hide carefully, and torture me day after day.

I realized that I "charmed" and attracted them in some "secret" way. I may not be able to say goodbye to these uninvited friends of mine, but knowing how to talk to and understand them helps me quickly gain insights into myself and find solutions to my challenges, and because of that, I have more time to spend with more pleasant emotions.

But why do I need to get rid of unpleasant emotions? The lessons they bring are invaluable gifts, offering me opportunities to grow every day, helping me love myself more, gain a better understanding of people around me, and live my life meaningfully.

That is my experience of uninvited emotional friends.

- ▶ *Which uninvited guests do you often attract?*
- ▶ *How are you "welcoming" them?*
- ▶ *What valuable lessons do they offer?*

DAN'S THOUGHTS

Stop for a moment and think about what you learned about emotions growing up.

Uninvited Emotional Friends

Universally my students report that they learned things like:

- Emotions cannot be trusted
- You need to control your emotions
- You should not display certain emotions
- Emotions are a sign of weakness
- Some emotions are positive and others are negative
- You can avoid or suppress your emotions
- Emotions get in the way of clear thinking and decision-making

Every human being has a large and similar palette of emotions. How each of us relates to and lives out those emotions differs. Our biology has a role to play, as does all that we learned from our parents, families, and culture. Then there are our many experiences and the way we've interpreted what they mean. Some emotions are easily accessible to us and some are a struggle to generate. Some we need to moderate and others to practice and strengthen. Nevertheless, each of us has an emotional toolbox to draw from.

An increasing body of research confirms that emotions are a domain of learning, that they are part of every aspect of our lives, and that most of us remain emotionally ignorant. The good news is that ignorance is curable through learning.

Begin by noticing. Stop what you are doing, turn your attention inside, and notice what you are feeling, the sensations in your body, the tension, your breathing, and your thoughts. Now, put the name of an emotion to all of that.

Hello Emotions!

Interestingly, even well-educated adults tend to use the same fifteen or twenty words to describe their emotions. We have a very small active emotional vocabulary. Expanding this is a fantastic place to begin your emotional learning. Distinctions give you expertise. A chef knows the differences between dozens of spices and herbs and which produce certain flavors. The same happens when we can name and understand sixty or eighty emotions clearly.

So, whether an emotion visits you often or rarely, learn to identify it, learn what it is trying to tell you and its purpose. You'll be amazed how useful your emotions can be in helping you create the life you desire.

EMOTIONS NEVER LIE

Becoming a coach is not an easy journey. I only learned that lesson after burning the bridges to my former life. There are many fascinating challenges, and one of the most compelling is to help my Ego shrink as much as possible.

In the past, Big Ego made me miserable. She demanded that once a goal was set, no matter what happened, I had to be the best. No one could be better. To be the best, she forced me to keep an eye on what others were doing and to envy or hate them. She expected whatever I said to be right and true, which made me nervous and worried every time I ran a workshop. I was afraid that someone would challenge what I was about to say and I would not be able to defend my argument.

After tasting enough suffering because of Big Ego, I promised myself to shrink her. Day after day I kept a close watch on her, until one day I felt that I no longer hated the people I used to hate, that I no longer had the urge to defend myself against others. It didn't matter whether I was better or worse than others, and I was able to smile calmly and accept opposing thoughts in my classes. Released from her grip, I thought, "Ego, you are finally getting smaller."

One morning, I awoke because someone was knocking on my door. A few minutes later, Anxiety rushed in with tension in her face: "Do you know what? It's been three years since the day you took your first step on this coaching road, and now there are too many people following this same route."

Ego tried to calm Anxiety down: "It doesn't matter, my friend. I no longer want to compete with anyone, so there is no need to worry about it. I stopped searching for and monitoring other coaches' fan pages a long time ago. I no longer hate anyone anymore. Don't worry."

"I know, but I am still worried." Anxiety didn't seem satisfied.

Leaving Anxiety sitting with all her worries in the corner of the room, I walked out into the yard. Someone stood at the door waiting for me.

"Oh, Sadness, why are you here? I rarely see you in the company of Anxiety. Tell me, did I miss something important?"

"Don't you remember? You've worked day and night, rarely resting, in the hope that you would soon reach the place where you could make a huge difference in the world and be a unique offer. With so many people on the same road now, how can you make your dream come true? You have lost your dream!" Sadness looked me in the eyes.

I was silent. Oh, so Ego, even though she had become smaller, was still strong enough to secretly sow her thoughts in my mind. She had been whispering in my ear that I was already at peace with a humble life, not asking for anything more, but deep inside there was still a desire to surpass everyone else, to become unique.

I breathed a sigh of relief, knowing what to do next with Ego.

I thanked Anxiety and Sadness for honestly sharing their thoughts with me. The two smiled and waved goodbye, leaving me sitting contentedly in my sunny courtyard.

- ▶ *Are you listening to your emotional friends?*
- ▶ *What is the truth they are trying to tell you?*
- ▶ *Do you judge them or do you listen to them as you would a trusted companion?*

DAN'S THOUGHTS

When we learn to trust that our emotions have our best interest at heart and that they exist to support us, we begin a new relationship with them. We stop doubting, fighting, and wrestling with them and begin to treat them with a newfound respect. We begin to see them as good friends.

I'm sure you have at least a few good friends. Think for a moment what your relationship with them entails. You usually enjoy their company, but not always. Sometimes they amuse you or make you laugh and at other times you find them annoying and would prefer to be alone. If they are good friends, though, they always have your best interest at heart and will be there to support you when you need them. They will not abandon you in your hour of need. This is the relationship we can develop with our emotions if we choose.

Befriending your emotions can be one of the most enlightening and powerful things you choose to do in your life. Because we've grown up with so many ineffective ways of understanding emotions, there is a tremendous territory to discover. So, what will it be? Will you continue to wrestle and fight with your emotions, expending energy unnecessarily, or will you begin to explore a new relationship with them that brings peace and harmony? It's up to you.

UNCOMFORTABLE EMOTIONS CARE

After a long day at work, when you are near exhaustion or when you get sick, which emotional friends are with you? In my case, they are always uncomfortable ones, namely Anxiety, Fear, Anger, or Hate, and the list goes on. They naturally appear, rushing into my house, telling me old stories in an attempt to "entertain" me during my difficulties.

Fear usually comes first, saying, "Hey, Thao, how are you feeling? Your headache seems severe this time. I think we should go to the hospital immediately to get a brain scan just in case. Lately, I've heard many young people suffer a stroke without noticing."

Indignation continues, "Do you remember that annoying email yesterday? I can't believe that they treated you that way. Do you want me to reply and restore justice?"

Hate shouts, "That would just waste our time, Indignation. Don't you see Thao isn't well? Let it go and just end the relationship with that person. I can't stand him anymore anyway!"

When we are weak, the presence of our loved ones is the best thing to have, isn't it? So while I appreciate their presence and that they come with good intentions, it is just too much for me.

In those moments, I long for other more comfortable companions such as Peace, Serenity, or Equanimity, but they never come until I focus on breathing, relaxing, and living in the moment. So I like to think difficult emotions are more caring.

Another big lesson I have learned during challenging times is to take care of my physical health. I discipline myself to do sitting meditation, go jogging every morning, and practice yoga in the evening. I eat healthy foods, spend time in nature, and rest often throughout the day. These activities help me have more time with comfortable emotions and spend less time being visited by uncomfortable ones.

- ▶ *"Who" is with you during your difficult moments?*
- ▶ *Which emotional friends do you have the impulse to run away from?*
- ▶ *What do you do to stay longer with your comfortable friends each day?*

DAN'S THOUGHTS

Whether an emotion is comfortable or uncomfortable has no relationship to its importance and utility. Anxiety is uncomfortable for most of us, but without it, we would not remain vigilant for possible danger. That would make us incredibly vulnerable. Resentment feels terrible, but it tells us something unfair is occurring and gives us the opportunity to take care of it.

The reason emotions feel pleasant or unpleasant is to get our attention. You'll notice that the emotions that trigger the strongest sensations are generally emotions that have some urgency or importance. If jealousy came calling with subtle sensations, we might not even notice it. It is the depth of the discomfort we feel that calls our attention.

Although an emotion like anger announces itself boldly, the experience interpreted by every person is not the same. Many people feel uncomfortable when anger shows up, but others enjoy the energy of it. This is another reason to be sure we don't fall into the habit of confusing the comfort or discomfort of an emotion with its meaning or value.

Hello Emotions!

EMOTIONS LOVE BREATHING

Emotions love breathing! This was a "shocking" discovery I made late one evening.

That day Fear arrived while my family was having dinner. She said, "Look, your mother is having a huge bowl of noodles with a pinch of herbs, seasoned with cane sugar. In a little while, your mother's blood sugar will spike beyond the acceptable range." My mother was keen to finish that whole bowl of noodles while I sat silently, taking each bite with Fear.

After dinner, I retreated to my bedroom and grabbed my favorite book, hoping Fear would get bored with the academic words I was reading and go elsewhere. But no, she sat patiently right beside me, her eyes fixed on each page reading with interest. Sitting next to Fear, my breaths became shorter and heavier with every passing minute. My heart beat faster and palpitated, my throat became constricted, and my shoulders tensed up. All of a sudden, it felt suffocating.

My eyes still saw each word, but the words did not register in my brain. Putting my book down, I focused on each in-and-out breath, feeling the rise and fall of my abdomen, the constriction in my chest, the choking in my throat, and the tension in my shoulders. Strangely, the more I focused on each unpleasant physical sensation, the more comfortable my body became. My breathing became deeper and gentler, my heart returned to its normal rhythm, and my neck relaxed. My body and mind were at ease. Looking over, I saw that Fear was dozing off.

Out of curiosity, I tried applying this method whenever Anger, Resentment, Disappointment, or another uncomfortable emotion came to visit. They were all lulled to sleep with cool, gentle, deep, slow breaths. When they woke up, they always shared insights into myself and lessons or solutions that I rarely had to "explain" later to Regret and Guilt.

Reflecting on it, I realize now that after each meditation session, my mind is always brighter, my energy more peaceful and placid, and I can "hear" the messages of my shyest emotional friends. Those are the guys who hide so well in some secret corner in my house, but always hold the key to my challenging situations.

Later, I was surprised to find that this "shocking" discovery is something many people in the world already know. If you search for the word Mindfulness on Amazon, more than 40,000 search results show up. If you search the website of Harvard Business Review, you will find numerous psychological studies on the relationship between Mindfulness and Emotional Intelligence.

I smiled joyfully and gratefully for the good fortune that had brought me the knowledge of Mindfulness and the world of my lovely emotional friends. This wonderful combination has helped me cherish all my emotions and learn countless valuable lessons about myself, thereby being able to love myself and the people around me a little more every passing day.

▶ *Do you notice that every emotion has a different breath pattern?*

▶ *Have you experimented with changing your breathing to shift an emotion?*

▶ *How could you practice aligning your emotions and your breath?*

DAN'S THOUGHTS

Butterflies in our stomach tell us we are feeling anxiety, and opening our eyes wide suggests surprise. Most of us are aware of a few connections between what we are sensing physically and our emotions, but many more are possible.

Thao's story highlights how the breath is connected directly with both generating and shifting emotions. This is an area in which one could spend a lifetime studying, experimenting, and making discoveries. In our "modern" world we often look to medication to resolve emotionally what mindfulness practices could if we understood and used them.

Hello Emotions!

How helpful would it be if you had a simple, self-implemented method for facing and moving through fear? What about anxiety, self-doubt, shame, or guilt? This is one benefit that building your emotional literacy and practicing mindfulness can give you. And it can be a "shocking" discovery when it begins to work for you.

UGLY OR BEAUTIFUL?

If one day
Anger no longer existed
How could we distinguish
Rightness, wrongness?
How could we fight for justice?
Is Anger ugly?
Yes! It is when
He kidnaps our mind

If one day
Fear no longer visited and
Danger awaited
How would we anticipate it?
Is Fear ugly?
Yes! She can be
When we surrender trembling
And not daring
To face her

Hello Emotions!

So we can, once again, see
A blue sky of hope

If one day
There was no Sadness
How could we understand
What we value in this life?
Is Sadness ugly?
Yes! If we only sit hugging her
Wallowing in our loss

If one day
Boredom became a stranger
How could we know
We have grown?
Is Boredom ugly?
Yes! It is when we
Miss its meaning
And become complacent

If one day
Regret became invisible
Who would remind us
"Don't make the same mistake"?
Is Regret ugly?

Ugly or Beautiful?

Yes! It is when
We let her torment us
Rather than teach us

If one day
Guilt turned into nothingness
How would we know our values?
Is Guilt ugly?
Yes! It is when we let him
Eat away our soul
Rather than celebrating who we are

If one day
Loneliness disappeared
How could we learn
To treasure friendship?
Is Loneliness ugly?
Yes! If we avoid seeking out
People to share life with

Emotions are ugly
or
Emotions are beautiful
The answer is in YOU!

DAN'S THOUGHTS

We each have a way of thinking about emotions. We have beliefs, opinions, and judgments about them. We even have emotions about our emotions.

Many of us grew up believing that emotions were a problem to be solved rather than a skill to be learned. When we see them this way, we often see them, or some of them, as ugly.

Nothing allows us to explore and learn about emotions more than suspending our judgments of them and simplifying seeing them as something that is. When we can simply say "I feel anxious" or "I feel joy" without judging either right or wrong, we will find a friend in our emotions.

As Thao says, "It is up to you!"

ACKNOWLEDGMENTS

THAO

I often think that I had been living in darkness for almost forty years until the day I "met" Thay Thich Nhat Hanh through his books and began to learn Mindfulness. It was one of the darkest moments in my life, when I had lost all sense of direction and more than once wondered if it was worth living. Each word in Thay's books seemed written for me. Sometimes they provoked delight and I wondered, "How can someone understand me so well?" Thay's simple but profound stories, full of wisdom, have gradually penetrated my heart, rescuing me from my island of ignorance.

Little by little, I started seeing the light of the sun through the practice of Mindfulness. The sunlight has been illuminating my path and has helped me see things I could not before. They are not new things. They have always existed and recurred in my daily life, but I just could not see them well and kept stumbling over them or banging my head on them in darkness. Thanks to my Mindfulness practice, I have started seeing clearly what is happening around me, and even more importantly, inside me. I definitely would not be able to "see" my emotional friends and tell their stories without a Mindfulness practice.

Thay is the person who inspired me to love emotions and take care of them with gentleness. Thay is also the person who has awakened my love of Buddha, who in turn has inspired me to be resilient on my path. I am truly grateful!

It is only a tiny gift, but I would like to present my part (half of the revenue of this book) to Thich Nhat Hanh Foundation and/or Plum Village. I truly hope Mindfulness can reach many more people.

I still remember the day I "met" Dan Newby. To be precise, it was an evening I joined a virtual session offered by the International Coaching Federation. Dan presented his coaching framework based on the understanding of the world of emotions. During his presentation, I felt as if I had stopped breathing and blinked my eyes to be sure they were open. My heart beat joyfully! "I've found the path" was what I believed at that moment. A few weeks later I was one of Dan's students in his Emotional Literacy training course. I have learned from Dan to distinguish and understand my emotional friends.

The combination of Mindfulness practice and knowledge of emotional literacy has helped me learn to have meaningful conversations with emotions and gain enormous insight into myself. I started sharing my stories with my communities and received great encouragement. One day, I emailed Dan, asking him if I could use parts of his book *The Field Guide to Emotions* in my first book. Dan was so generous as to let me use whatever I would like to. And when I became discouraged and almost gave up my dream of writing a book, once again Dan was the one who encouraged me to pursue it. Dan has also helped restore the soul of the original Vietnamese version from Trinh's and my draft translations. I have learned so much from Dan on this co-writing journey. My stories in the book, therefore, would not be here without the knowledge, wisdom, guidance, support, and encouragement of Dan, one of my greatest teachers so far! Thank you so much, Dan! I am grateful!

You may notice there are a few questions for further contemplation after each story. I have learned how to craft those questions from the Ontological Coach Training Program of The Coach Partnership. So I am grateful for being trained by my wonderful teachers, including Mark Hemstedt, Marcus Marsden, Terrie Lugberger, Chris Balsley, Jim Smith, Beatriz Garcia, and many other Master Coaches whom I have learned from through their books and blogs. I include Carly Anderson and Doug Silsbee.

There are some friends whom it is hard for us to "let leave" our life because they insist on being with us during our hard times. For me, Trinh Nguyen is the one. She has been with me through all the storms that have swept through my life, although she always refuses to enjoy the rainbow with me after the storm has passed. It has happened a few times, and this time I am determined not to let it be repeated. So your name is in this book, Trinh. I am truly grateful for being your friend, for having your support and encouragement for more than ten years. And thank you for helping to translate part of my stories. I hope you found this journey as fun and enjoyable as I did.

The Mindfulness Lovers group, which includes Thu Le, Hang Ngo, Nham Nguyen, Yen Hoang, Lien Hoang, Hanh Ngo, Phuong Truong, Thu Do, and Ngoc Nguyen. Although we only found each other about a year ago and all come from different backgrounds, it feels like we are destined to be on the same road, strolling toward the same destination. You are the ones who help me stay disciplined with my Mindfulness practice. I am grateful!

My close friends, including An Luong, Hang Thai, Giang Do, Vu Tran, Phuong Le, Ha Tran, Quang Le, Thong Pham, and anh Thien Tran. Your jokes, funny photos, useful tips, and presence have lightened my days for more than a decade and counting. I am grateful to be part of our small family.

Thao Huong Vu and Tuan Anh Vu. Do you remember numerous evenings we spent together to share our experiences and knowledge about the emotional and coaching world? These conversations helped me feel much less lonely on the very first days on my journey. Thank you so much for being my cheerleaders, beloved friends, and strategic consultants when it comes to marketing ideas. I am truly grateful!

Chi Ngan Ly, chi Nguyet Tran, Tuong Phan and Thao Phan. Your message "How are you? I notice you have stopped writing and sharing on your Facebook ..." was one of my sources of energy to reach this first milestone. Your care means so much to me. I am grateful!

A heartfelt thanks to Debbie Yow. You are the one who gave me the opportunity to be exposed to the world of coaching. And do you remember our conversation four years ago at lunch? I was deeply touched by your prayer for my coaching journey. I am so grateful!

To all my friends, ex-colleagues, ex-bosses, clients (many now are friends), and Facebook friends who have been reading my stories, sincere thanks for your generous support with comments, feedback, and encouragement during this four-year journey.

In gratitude,
Thao

DAN

Collaborating on this book has been a great joy for me. Although Thao cites me as her teacher, in writing this book she has been mine. I have learned a great deal about the lyricism and personality of emotions. I've gained insights into my emotions and the relationships they have with each other.

Thao, I thank you for the invitation to join you on this journey and for trusting me with your dream, your baby. I am honored.

One of the other collaborators I've journeyed with these past years is my wife, Lucy Núñez. She has co-written and translated three books with me and helps me every day to question and refine my understanding of emotions. She has helped me grow emotionally, and I'm grateful for our relationship in its many dimensions daily.

I would be remiss not to mention the source of some of the key emotional principles I work with if I did not thank Rafael Echeverria and Julio Olalla for their teaching. They helped me find the path to building my emotional literacy and ways to begin articulating it for others. Without their wisdom, I would not be where I find myself today. My deepest appreciation to you both.

Finally, I want to thank my students. Their questions, challenges, insights, and observations continually show me what I don't know and prompt me to find new ways to understand and explain emotions. Along with my observations of me and the world around me, they are my biggest teachers. It would be impossible to name you all, but I am nevertheless grateful to each of you.

Life and emotions are gifts. I don't know how or why these gifts came, but I am grateful. I don't know the source of these gifts, but feel wonder and awe when I realize their magnitude. Once, I wished I could rid myself of my emotions. Now I rue the day I will no longer be able to explore them. But, I understand that is the cycle of life and death, and I both embrace and accept it. Let us enjoy the journey wherever it takes us and as long as it lasts.

Warmly,

Dan

Hello Emotions!

ABOUT THE AUTHORS

THAO PHAM

Thao is a coach, a trainer, and the CEO at overflowingbuckets. com. She holds a Professional Certified Coach credential from the International Coaching Federation, is a Newfield Certified Coach from The Coach Partnership, as well as a Gallup-Certified Strengths Coach. Thao began her career as a Research and Development specialist in 2004. After two years, she discovered that her first love was really market research and moved into that industry for the next ten years, working with Nielsen, Unilever Vietnam, and Unilever Asia Private Ltd. In her last role at Unilever as Consumer and Market Insights Senior Manager 2C, where she took charge of the entire Laundry category in Southeast Asia and Australia, she developed a deep understanding of people and their insights and aspirations in life. This was core to her embarking on her journey in coaching at the end of 2017. A native of Vietnam, Thao had also lived in Australia and Singapore for five years. She is a strong believer in mindfulness and is passionate about helping people love themselves a little more every day.

DAN NEWBY

Dan is a native of the United States, the son of a Protestant minister and teacher. His worldview was shaped by living many of his developmental years in Central Africa and Switzerland. Later, he had the opportunity to live in the Middle East, Italy, Malta, and now Spain. He trained as a teacher and worked in a variety of roles in business, including project manager, divisional leader, COO, and CEO. For the past twenty years, he has been a coach, coach trainer, teacher, and writer. He is the founder of The School of Emotions and co-author of four books: *The Unopened Gift: A Primer in Emotional Literacy*, *21 Days to Emotional Literacy*, *The Field Guide to Emotions*, and *The Journey Inside: Coaching to the Core*.

Dan envisions a world in which we embrace emotions rather than seeing them as something we need to hide, control, or be embarrassed about. Dan's love for this topic emerged from his realization that emotional ignorance was at the root of many difficulties in his life and that all humans are emotional beings.